Path to

Enlightenment
The Pillar of Light

Nasrin Safai

BOOK I

Waves of Bliss Publishing

Book design: Yantra Design Group, Inc.

Photography: ©Patsy Balacchi

Diagrams created by Theresa Martin, Michael Kopel, Tonia-Maria Pinheiro

Path to Enlightenment, Book I. Waves of Bliss Publishing, 2008.
ISBN 978-0-9821302-0-9
Library of Congress Control Number: 2008937865

Waves of Bliss Publishing, Jeffersonville, VT 05464
To order books:
    Email: Nasrin@WavesOfBliss.com
    Website: www.wavesofbliss.com/books

Other books by Nasrin Safai:
Path to Enlightenment, Book II, Waves of Bliss Publishing 2008

Path to Enlightenment, Book III, Waves of Bliss Publishing 2008

Gifts from Ascended Beings of Light: Prayers, Meditations, Mantras and Journeys for Soul Growth – Gifts I. Agapi Publishing, 2003.

Gifts of Practical Guidance for Daily Living: Protection, Healing, Manifestation, Enlightenment – Gifts II. Waves of Bliss Publishing, 2005.

Gifts from the Masters of Light: Journeys Into the Inner Realms of Consciousness – Gifts III. Waves of Bliss Publishing, 2005.

Gifts of Wisdom and Truth from the Masters of Light: Tools for Clearing, Release, Abundance and Empowerment – Gifts IV. Waves of Bliss Publishing, 2005.

Altered States, Biographies & Personal Experience, Body Mind & Spirit, Chakras, Channeling, Consciousness: Awareness & Expansion, Creation Spirituality, Daily Meditation, Everyday Spirituality, God, Meditation & Prayer, New Age, Origin & Destiny of Individual Souls, Science & Religion, Spiritual Teachers, Spirituality, Self Help, The Self.

Printed in the United States of America.

KEY TERMS

TO ENHANCE YOUR READING EXPERIENCE

What is offered to you through these books is the result of three decades of accumulated knowledge on my part and thousands of hours worth of ageless wisdom delivered by the Masters. This book is therefore written as a multi-layered exercise. Reading this book affects you at conscious and sub-conscious levels. To enhance your experience and to get the most out of reading this book, please follow these recommendations:

Start by saying:

- *"In the name of Light, I ask that I experience the utmost benefit that this book can offer me at conscious and sub-conscious levels. I call upon my Personal Guides and Guardian Angels to be present through the course of reading this book. I invite the Angelic Forces of Light, the Masters of Light, and the Great Beings of Light to administer to me the highest benefit from their energy and their teachings through this book."*

- Read the Introduction carefully as it provides the key which opens the doors to the understanding of the chapters that follow. The foundation for many of the concepts discussed in each chapter is created by the framework provided in the Introduction.

- It is my opinion that if you walk away from each of the books in this series with a good knowledge of what is presented in the introduction, with clear objectivity, you would have accelerated yourself on the Path to Enlightenment.

- Even though this book is an attempt to be the first step on the path of Enlightenment, some knowledge of esoteric teachings, spiritual studies both ancient and new and awareness of the work of the Ascended Masters is recommended. To gain a greater knowledge of this subject, please refer to the books in the *Gifts* series by Nasrin Safai.

- After you read this book from cover to cover you may still feel that you have not fully understood everything completely. Do not be concerned, as a period of time for introspection and reflection will bring things to focus. The moment you pick up any one of these books, you begin to walk with the Masters and receive their teachings at subconscious levels. In time, you will consciously understand their wisdom. You may surprise yourself as to how much of this wisdom you retain and use in your everyday lives.

- It is my intention to present you with information and materials directly given by the Masters whom I channel. The Masters feel that understanding the subject consciously and energetically through them as the source will help the assimilation process. Once you have made your connection with them, and assimilate their teachings, they will lead you to more on that subject when you ask for it. In that way, you will be lead to what is most pertinent and beneficial for you without confusion or delays. I have therefore kept the quotes and materials from other sources to an absolute minimum. However, for those of you interested in reading more on some of these topics, I provide a short bibliography at the end of the book. These external sources have been mentioned in my *Gifts* series books with greater detail at pertinent points in the text.

THE GREAT INVOCATION

From the point of Light within the mind of God
Let Light stream forth into the minds of men.
Let Light descend on Earth.

From the point of Love within the heart of God
Let Love stream forth into the hearts of men.
May Christ return to Earth.

From the center where the Will of God is known
Let purpose guide the little wills of men -
The purpose which the Masters know and serve.

From the center which we call the race of men
Let the Plan of Love and Light work out
And may it seal the door where evil dwells.

Let Light and Love and Power
Restore the plan on Earth.

Christ Maitreya, the World Teacher, and the Masters of Wisdom highly recommend that we recite the prayer of The Great Invocation daily. It transmits the energies of great Light, peace and harmony.

PREFACE

This is a channeled book. The information presented here has been channeled through me by the Ascended Masters of Light from the Higher Dimensional Realms. These realms are the abode of Enlightened people who have mastered the art of living in the density of this third dimensional reality and have graduated from it to Higher Realms. Their guidance, advice and support are available to us in this Third Dimensional reality. Those who can connect to the Higher Realms and see or hear the Masters are known to have psychic abilities.

I became aware of the Higher Realms very early in my life or should say I was aware of the existence of a world which was apparently known to me but not to most others. Throughout my adolescence and young adulthood, I struggled to understand how my psychic abilities could and should be brought into focus and used to serve a higher purpose. It was not an easy time or an easy process. I was living in the mundane world fraught with problems, trials and tribulations with a foot in the world of the sublime, which had its own challenges. I have always loved God desperately and intensely. Through constant prayer and pleas for help to God, I was able to harness my psychic abilities, develop a connection with the Ascended Masters, roam in the Higher Realms and become a channel. I was taught by the Masters and have developed my own style over the years. As the body of channeled material builds up, my awareness and understanding of the vast resources available to us in the Higher Realms extends.

This is not a book about channeling, but it is the purpose of this book to present wisdom and healing that has come directly from the Masters during channeling sessions. The sessions that this material was taken from happened over the years of 2004 through 2008.

WHAT IS CHANNELING?

Channeling is an energy dynamic which commonly involves at least three beings. The first is the channel who is the vehicle to receive the information. The channel has the ability to become the voice, the hands, the eyes, the ears, and the body of the Master for a short period of time. The second is the Ascended Master who allows his/her voice and energy to be heard and felt through the channel by the recipient. That recipient, also known as the student or disciple, is the third person in this equation whom the channeling session is conducted for. Even though I am able to see, hear and speak to the Masters on my own, it is not the same as when others are present. There is a significant difference between Metatron talking to me in the Inner Realms and embodying me in a channeling session.

When the Masters are held in my body, they are connected to this third dimensional realm through my body. They can send their healing energies and impart their wisdom directly to the recipients and the healing and wisdom can be received, with tangible and palpable impact. In special circumstances, to receive information for a book or newsletter, I have channeled for myself. In effect, I was both channel and recipient. In either case, the wisdom is dispensed and the energies of the Masters are embraced in this third dimension where we most need it. Our conscious understanding can absorb and digest the teachings and use it to enhance our lives and the lives of others.

It is important to note that there is a stated or implied agreement between all participants of a channeling session; the channel, the recipient and the Master. The channeling session comes about through a desire from all parties to be elevated by the contents to greater Light and wisdom and for the information to be used in service to the Light for the good of all. The intent to serve in this way plays an important role in holding the energy in focus, allowing smooth and clear communication with the Master. The channel is serving as the vehicle for the transmission of knowledge from the Master to recipients. The person who has requested the channeling is providing the service of "asking to receive" from the Master and helping to hold space for the channel. The Master imbues each word of his or her discourse with potent energies of Love, Healing and Higher Light. Great wisdom is dispersed through the teachings, which can benefit all humankind. Each healing and all wisdom given in a session, even though it may be given to only one person, is needed by and offered for the benefit of the multitudes and masses as well as Mother Earth.

Even when the channeling is being conducted over the phone, the effect is the same as if they were next to me. The phone connects me to the person verbally and energetically. This connection is being held in the third dimension, yet from the Masters' point of view, their energetic connection is not dictated by time and space. They can just as easily be sitting by your side, administering a healing while they are channeling the information through me.

To understand the channeling process, it is important to know the effects that channeling has on the physical body of the channel. When I channel, my consciousness literally steps aside and allows one of the Masters to energetically occupy my body. In doing this, my consciousness sits aside and quietly watches and listens to the exchange. I do not go into a trance to receive the information. The phrase trance-medium or trance-channel refers to a person who goes into a trance while channeling. Such a person, therefore, does not remain consciously aware of the channeling event. Since I am a conscious channel, I have an intended and controlled out of body experience. This out of body experience is a separation of my soul from my personality and my physical body, which is not necessarily appreciated by my personality or my physical body. My consciousness fully enjoys the experience of being embraced by my soul and by the Masters. However, when the session is over and I come back to my body, I may have an irritated mind and an emotionally rebellious personality to contend with, not to mention a physical body weary from having intense energies blasting through it, sometimes for hours at a time. It sometimes takes me several hours and occasionally a few days to settle back in my body.

WHY READ A CHANNELED BOOK
ABOUT ENLIGHTENMENT?

To read about any subject we go to those who have mastered that subject and are experts at it. To read on Enlightenment, we would want to go to Enlightened people. However, the majority of people who reach Enlightenment leave this reality behind. This is because their work is complete. It is our goal as human beings and our destiny as God-beings to reach Enlightenment, individually and en-mass. When we do, we are done. We leave to go to the Higher Realms and serve the Higher Light. Once there, some choose to serve the Light by becoming Masters and guides to those who are left behind in the third dimensional realms. It is these Masters, or so called Ascended Masters, who come through during channeling sessions. Their knowledge of Enlightenment is a proven fact, their ability to teach us the ropes is a given.

They too will have to study when in the Higher Realms to become teachers and guides, especially when specializing in such an advanced topic as Enlightenment. Then they train their disciples here on Earth. The trained disciple then becomes the vehicle or the channel to bring forth the knowledge and information. There are universal laws governing how such information is dispersed and restrictions which apply to these laws.

This is why clear and concise information on such a topic as Enlightenment is scarce. Much of the information is cloaked in poetry or prose or given in the forms of parables and riddles which can only be deciphered by serious and highly elevated students and high level initiates. In the past, such knowledge has been dispersed in Mystery Schools to high level initiates of the Mysteries, also called the occult. Such information is dispersed orally over many years to the students, who are sworn to secrecy in order to maintain the integrity of these teachings and to protect them from falling upon undeserving hands. The time has finally arrived when the Masters are choosing to make this material available to all seekers through these books.

On rare occasions and in special circumstances, an Enlightened being agrees to stay behind to serve others, to touch the masses with their Light or to just be the Beacons of Light illuminating this third dimensional reality. These are the living Masters. Those among them who choose to be the Beacons of Light may go into hiding from the masses simply to maintain their focus on holding the Light. We may not know them even if they lived next door to us. Others, who focus on people, continue to touch the multitudes and masses. Much of their time goes to traveling the world and reaching out to people. Many know them as spiritual teachers, living Masters, saints, gurus and avatars. People who choose to serve in their discipleship follow them, listening to every tidbit of information and taking it to heart.

These are the living Masters. Those among them who choose to be the Beacons of Light may go into hiding from the masses simply to maintain their focus on holding the Light. We may not know them even if they lived next door to us. Others, who focus on people, continue to touch the multitudes and masses. Much of their time goes to traveling the world and reaching out to people. Many know them as spiritual teachers, living Masters, saints, gurus and avatars. People who choose to serve in their discipleship follow them, listening to every tidbit of information and taking it to heart.

Among the living Masters who do stay behind to serve, the avatars are the most rare with the brightest Light, capable of carrying and spreading such Light to the greatest number of followers. Avatars are born Enlightened. They simply come to bring their Light and their teachings to us. Their life is an act of selfless sacrifice and their presence a blessing to Earth and all humankind.

Contending with a world full of people, six and a half billion strong, with almost all deeply and desperately in need of love and healing, these living Masters and avatars have the hardest task of all. For every student consciously seeking Enlightenment, there are thousands, even hundreds of thousands who are needy of a touch, a hug, a word, a glance. Their time and their energy go into appeasing these needs of the Majority. Their teachings, for the most part, become simple messages of hope and extension of love. Some even take vows of silence in order to place the emphasis on healing and imbuing the masses with Light rather than with words.

In my *Gifts* books series, I speak of a handful of such rare and amazing beings. These are the ones whom I have had the good fortune of receiving blessings first hand. I make a point of announcing in my newsletters and informing people in group sessions of their appearances and world tour schedules.

With that said, what remains in terms of materials available to aid the serious students of Enlightenment along the path are scarce. With this in view, the Masters of Light who guide me have chosen to provide first hand materials in the form of meditational exercises, grids of Light, candle grids, ceremonies, mantras, prayers, decrees and invocations which are presented to you in three books, all of which will go into print simultaneously. Each book will add greater force, intensity and acceleration, building momentum for faster results.

The world needs those who are seriously pursuing a spiritual path to be accelerated as this is a time when Earth is choosing the path of Enlightenment as her own destiny. Mother Earth needs us to pave the path for others to follow and lift the density from the surface of her body, to make her burden lighter and the path of Enlightenment illuminated. To facilitate this, I was instructed by the Masters to prepare this material.

The goal of this book and others in this series is to pave the path for the true seekers and the sincere students of Enlightenment. The tools presented are intended for all who are willing to serve in discipleship of the Masters and in service to the Light. These teachings aim to accelerate the students and disciples on their path to Enlightenment in the hope that once reached; they would devote their lives to serving Earth and all souls.

I wish you a great and fulfilling journey on the path to Enlightenment.

Narsin Safai
August 8, 2008
Miami Beach, Florida

INTRODUCTION

This book came about on two parallel courses. One was the course my colleagues and I took to get here, the other was the course the Masters took, which I was oblivious to, until I sat down to pull the chapters together.

The original idea for this book came up as a twelve steps to enlightenment concept. The thought was to use the twelve months of a calendar year as a format, since most of the exercises I present in the book are to be repeated for twenty two days, or about a month. We could use the exercises which were given in our monthly newsletters published on many different topics for such a book. When I sat down with the Masters to get their direction, I found out about the parallel course they had taken. They quickly showed me that the newsletters compiled over the last three years, un-be known to me, had been done in a step-by-step manner as if preparing the reader for Enlightenment. The order for a great step-by-step process for reaching Enlightenment was there all the time. The Masters requested that I combine these with some material from my previous books, the *Gifts* series, in order for the reader to receive the energetic benefits of both. With some editing, I have taken the newsletters from 2006 to the present and compiled three books which contain information, meditational Light Grids, exercises and Candle Grids. These can be effectively used by any sincere student of Enlightenment.

The books in this series are written for serious seekers whose goal is to consciously walk the path of Enlightenment. Such a seeker is therefore expected to have some prior knowledge of the basic concepts and definitions. The definitions and perspective that these books and my web site have, is quite predictably that of the Masters who channel through me. By taking this journey with the Masters through reading these books, you can find out how this material resonates with you. The information provided is meant to offer a solid foundation to prepare for Enlightenment. Determination, patience and perseverance are important requirements. After all, the goal does justify the means and is, in and of itself, an end.

WHAT IS ENLIGHTENMENT?

Enlightenment is a process. What I have learned is that Enlightenment is not a magical point in time where all is revealed and one becomes an instant avatar. It is a process. Having said that, there is a great event, a special moment in time which marks the point where the doors to Enlightenment open.

The mechanics of this process is that every human being is a conglomerate of many personality aspects. Higher Self, Lower Self, Male Aspect, Female Aspect, Child Aspect, Conscious Self and Soul Aspects make up the collective consciousness of an Incarnate Soul. When an individual's personality aspects become willing to accept integration with the soul aspects and the soul aspects with the personality aspects, the point is reached and Enlightenment begins. This is a critical step toward Oneness; when the soul and personality aspects agree to work together. The struggle for spiritual growth ends when the internal strife between Soul and Personality Aspects comes to a close.

Every meditation, every Light grid and every spiritual exercise offered to you in this book is aimed at bringing the personality and soul closer together. Over time, as they begin to have harmony, the consciousness begins to take its rightful neutral position as a witness to the play acted out by the personality and the soul aspects. As the consciousness gains neutrality, it feels calmer and the voice of the Higher Self becomes more discernable. The person becomes aware of the presence and teachings of the Higher Self. In time, the voice of the Higher Self, the True Self, can be fully adhered to. The Individual Will merges with the Will of the True Self and becomes the Divine Will.

There are an infinite number of routs to take on the path of Enlightenment and all of them are valid. Every soul will have its own unique way to experience the journey because everyone's contract is different. We have each agreed to our Soul Mission before taking this incarnation. The requirements of this contract dictate the path we will take to Enlightenment. For instance, there are living avatars such as Mother Meera, Sri Karunamayi, Ammachi and Sai Baba who are born Realized or Enlightened. This means that the veil which separates past from present and future is lifted. They can see and know anything they choose. They can also manifest anything in this third dimensional reality. Their contracts are to serve humankind in all the ways they do, each in their own unique style. Just by being incarnate on Earth and holding their great Light in this dimension of reality they provide great service. Yet even these beloved avatars are here on Earth because will grow and gain greater levels of Enlightenment.

The journey on the path to Enlightenment is an infinite one. There is always a greater level of Enlightenment available, a greater level of Oneness to experience and greater degrees of merging with the Divine. As the Dalai Lama, the leader of Tibet once said when asked if he had achieved Enlightenment, *"I am walking on that path."*

THE PILLAR OF LIGHT

To accelerate on the Path of Enlightenment, we need to raise our Quotient of Light. While we live in the density of this third dimensional reality, raising our vibration of Light and maintaining it becomes a challenge unless we have higher dimensional tools to assist us. One such tool is the Pillar of Light, also known as the Tube of Light or the Cylinder of Light.

The Pillar of Light is a higher dimensional energy field of Light. When called to form around our body, it can accelerate our spiritual growth by increasing our Quotient of Light and maintaining it at those levels. When the Pillar is fully formed and you reside inside of it permanently, you can remain detached from all fears, including fear of failure, loneliness, separation and rejection. When you are inside the Pillar of Light, you are directly connected to the Perfected Presence of the I AM THAT I AM, God in Form. This is the individualized presence of God which has taken form and resides at the thirteenth dimension of reality. Through your twelfth chakra, you are able to connect with this dimension and experience the perfected presence of the I AM THAT I AM. As expressed in chapter three of this book, in the wise words of Archangel Michael, *"This is perhaps the most important step in returning to the perfection of our Original Divine Plan. The Divine Plan as originally intended by God was to allow you to remain connected to God and to the Pure White Light at all times and in all circumstances."*

This is why the title of this book carries the all-important signature of the "Pillar of Light".

PERSONALITY ASPECTS

To gain a basic understanding of personality aspects and soul aspects, the Masters say that the body is the vehicle for the soul and the soul is the vehicle for the spirit. The body and small self is the realm of the personality aspects. We are all aware of a quality that is vaguely referred to as our personality. Usually, it is spoken of in the singular which connotes that we each have a personality, a general disposition. We define ourselves and others by our tendencies; how we act in different circumstances, how we handle pressure, how we express our emotions and our intellect. However, these are, in fact, qualities of the collective consciousness, of not one, but many of our personality aspects.

From the teachings of the Masters, we have learned that it is common to have up to twelve personality aspects definable and distinct from each other. The wants and needs of each are specific. Some have been with us through many incarnations while evolving to attain Higher Light. Others may have joined us for the first time in this incarnation. These aspects too reach their own level of Enlightenment and move on. New aspects replace them at new incarnations. Each lifetime we have one or two dominant personalities. Life is easier when the personality aspects get along with one another and when there is only one dominant personality, accepted and obeyed by all others.

Most of us are familiar with one of the personality aspects known as the Inner Child, sometimes also known as the Lower Self. This personality is an extremely important one as the gateway to the Higher Self can only be opened through the will of this aspect.

LEVELS OF INITIATION

There are landmark points that provide a yardstick for growth toward Enlightenment. The Hierarchy of the Masters has established Levels of Initiation as important landmark events in the journey of each soul on the path to Enlightenment and beyond. From the teachings of the Masters in various channelings, I am able to sum up and simplify the basic premise for each level of initiation up to the point of Enlightenment.

Before I move to the explanation of the initiates, I must make a distinction between the state of an un-awakened soul and an initiate. An un-awakened soul is a person who has no desire to partake of the Mysteries and no curiosity about what may lie behind the Mundane. The purpose of life and what may be in store after this life is of no interest to this person. Although deeply immersed in the Mundane, an un-awakened soul finds no yardstick to measure the dross and the pain of the Mundane and has no means for choosing to remove it.

A newly awakened soul would be one who becomes an initiate. This is someone whose curiosity has led to the search for the meaning of life and the greater purpose which lies behind. Such a person has become a seeker of knowledge and wisdom which would lead to the discovery of the Mysteries and to levels of initiation. A newly awakened soul, although still immersed in the Mundane, is looking to make changes to lift up the burden of the dross.

An initiate is someone who has chosen to study and pursue spiritual practices and, therefore, is a student of the mysteries. A Mystery School is a place where, once accepted, the student learns the

Mysteries or the secrets which enhance and accelerate them on the path to Enlightenment. Such students are sworn to secrecy and the Mystery Teachings are meant to be kept hidden from the non-initiates. Most Mystery Schools throughout history have passed the teachings orally from teachers to students in order to maintain the secrecy and the integrity of the teachings. Such is the importance attributed to states of initiation and the responsibility of being the bearer of the knowledge and wisdom held within.

A first level initiate is one who has awakened their Divine Spark, and has learned enough about the subject to treat it as more than just a curiosity or a hobby. This person is looking to seriously pursue the subject and is searching for a teacher who would point out the path to follow. The pursuit of the purpose and further meaning of life and their Divine Mission is a serious endeavor. At this point, though still immersed in the mundane, the initiate is making changes to be freed from the act of survival in the mundane and is ready and willing to let go of the pain and the dross.

A second level initiate, through self awareness and study, would have a stronger understanding of the Spiritual Realms, the Teachers, Guides and the Masters. They would be applying greater discipline in pursuing a specific path which they have consciously chosen. At this point, the initiate has one foot in the sublime and another in the mundane.

By the time an initiate reaches the third level, they would willingly offer their lives in service to the Light and for the good of all. At this level, the initiate has the full understanding that the purpose of this life is to serve and is only happy when they can do so. Life is lived as an act of service. Survival issues no longer create obstacles on the path of such an initiate because she/he has become empowered to be detached from worldly pursuits. In the wise sayings of our beloved Master Jesus, such an initiate, *"Is in the world but not of it."* This does not mean that worldly pursuits and empowerment in the mundane are not important, it simply means that the initiate has reached the point where they are capable of fulfilling all their needs with little or no distraction from the task at hand.

A fourth level initiate has reached the point in their spiritual evolution where they can roam the realms and can commune with the Masters and Great Beings. They have fully discovered their Divine Mission and are serving that mission from day to day. The fourth level initiate can be considered a full disciple of the Masters. Their personal will has by now begun to dissolve into the Divine Will and the Microcosm has become the holographic image of the Macrocosm, where the drop carries all the qualities of the ocean.

At around the fifth level, an initiate reaches Mastery. At this point, they may have a large group of followers, if their path is that of a teacher. As a Master, the initiate has accumulated knowledge and powers received directly from their Masters and from the elder brothers and sisters from their own soul grouping, or Soul Lineage. Each initiate now has direct access to the power and might of their entire Soul Lineage of Light. The power and might that each initiate will be able to bring forth into this lifetime depends on their karma, their contract or soul mission and many other important factors including their ability to earn the required merits. From this point on the Master initiate walks the path of self-realization, also known as God-realization or Enlightenment.

This is a crude and oversimplified description of the levels of initiation applicable to this present juncture in the history of Earth. There have been times in the evolution of souls on Earth where reaching mastery at the fourth level of initiation was the norm. Even though these norms create a framework for such generalities to exist, every individual is unique in their choices and therefore in the way in which they walk their path to reach Enlightenment. There are universal laws governing each level and protective measures which dictate and guard these rules. The Hierarchies of Ascended Masters and Great Beings sit upon governing boards leading initiates of each level on their path to greater evolution.

FRAMEWORK

Jeshua Ben Joseph was the given name of Jesus, which literally means Jeshua, son of Joseph. He introduces himself to us as Jeshua Ben Joseph in our channeling sessions. In Chapter I you are lead to first open your Third Eye as this is the window through which you can connect to the Inner Realms. Master Jesus does this through a guided meditation on a journey to Atlantis. Many souls, who were incarnate at some point during the civilization of Atlantis, chose to shut their Third Eye. This was the result of the pain and struggles endured in those Atlantean lifetimes. Chances are that you may be such a soul. The conscious or sub-conscious choices made in those lifetimes, during the destruction cycle of Atlantis, are still affecting us today. To regain the inner sight, to connect to the Higher Realms and to return to the original perfection, some of those decisions and choices must be reversed.

Master Jesus takes us on this meditational journey guiding us with utmost gentleness to awaken the memories and to choose to reverse the shutting of our Third Eye. He introduces us, in the process, to our Planetary Logos, Sanat Kumara. Logos means *"word"*. Sanat Kumara is the *"word"* for our planet. His consciousness over-lights this entire planet, including all souls and the planet herself. He has been a Father to this planet for the past 18½ million years. Our maternal parents, we only know and commune with in one lifetime. We choose different parents as we incarnate in each lifetime. Sanat Kumara has told us in channeling sessions that he shall continue for another 102 million years, give or take a few, to fulfill a 125 million year cycle. After this 125 million year cycle, Sanat Kumara will move on to bigger and better things. Therefore, for all intents and purposes, it would be safe to say that he is indeed our Eternal Father. Even though from a larger perspective, 125 million years may not fully constitute an eternity, it does for us, who live an average of 70-80 years at a time.

Our planet is one of free will. This means we are free to will ourselves to do as we wish. This is both a blessing and a curse. Our beloved Eternal Father, Sanat Kumara, the Hierarchies of Cosmic Beings and the God-Source, have given us permission to abandon ship, the ship of eternal union where we resided in Oneness in Heavenly Realms, to explore the flora and fauna of this magical planet we have come to know as our Mother Earth. Just as we were leaving ship, our Father, Sanat Kumara, said to us, *"Are you sure you want to do this?"* And we replied, *"Yes, we want to explore."* He replied, *"Do as you wish, remember to call if you need me. I will not bother you unless I hear from you."* And we said, *"Don't worry, we can manage."* He worried and we managed as best we could until now. This little anecdote, although an over-simplified version of the events, pretty much demonstrates what happened and how we came to have free will.

In the process of falling into the web of this world, we forgot our greatness and fell prey to our desires and the limitation of this third dimensional density. After eons of time, we are yearning for and longing to return to the unlimited, uninhibited World of Light and Spirit of Oneness. To accelerate ourselves on the path of return to Oneness, we must ask for help. It is true that our Father, the Planetary Logos and other Cosmic Beings of Light, know where we are and how we are faring. However, we did ask to be left alone. There should be no guilt or shame in calling for help. After all, is this not what our parents would do for us, as we would do for our children? The point is that we must first remember who we are and where we belong. Then we can ask for help, guidance and acceleration. To pave a pathway for our return journey we need the help of our beloved eternal parents, and God-parents like Sanat Kumara, Metatron and our older siblings like Master Jesus and Archangel Michael.

To prepare us to return to that state of Oneness which we had before we separated from them, in Chapter II, Master Jesus offers us a meditational exercise to cleanse and clear all the chakras of our bodies. The chakras are energy centers which connect our dense physical body to the more subtle and fluid energy bodies which, together with the physical body, create our wholeness. Over eons of time we have forgotten that we too are great beings. We are not merely this dense physical body but we also possess four layers of energy bodies. These additional layers around our physical body are invisible to the naked eye. Their purpose is to connect us to a greater reality. A reality which is limitless compared to what we experience through our physical body. They are, in order from the physical body outward: The etheric body, the emotional body, the mental body and the spiritual body. These layers, or energy bodies, are connected to our physical body through points of energy or chakras. Please refer to diagram on page 22.

Chakra, in Sanskrit means wheel. These energy centers literally operate like wheels. When these wheels are turning, the connection with our four outer energy bodies is maintained. When they are not turning, the connection stops. When it stops, we fail in communicating with these layers and remain unaware of their state. We therefore deprive ourselves of the resources available to us through each of these energy bodies. For example, our etheric body covers the physical body like an energetic blanket. The ability to remember the past and know the future, the ability to read another person's energy and intent is imprinted on the etheric body, also known as the auric body. Our instincts and intuition are heightened when our auric body is active and our auric field is clear. Kirlian photography shows different colored lights emanating from the auric body. From the cloud-burst of color registered in the photograph, a person trained in the art of aura reading can read your aura and examine your mood and state of health.

There are three more complex and higher vibrational layers of energy bodies beyond the etheric body. Each of these has their own role to play. The emotional body is the abode of all the feelings and emotions. It carries the memories of all events which have affected us emotionally, over time. Some fears and phobias are scars left from past events etched into this energy body. If there is no apparent cause for an event in this lifetime, you may be carrying a scar from a previous one, e.g. fear of drowning, fear of darkness, claustrophobia, etc.

The mental body is the abode of all thoughts and mental expressions. Every experience which has ever stimulated and given rise to a thought of any kind is held within this body. Imagine how powerful our minds could be if we were able to remember everything that has happened to us since our birth; and multiply that by the number of births we have had. Our brain has a much greater capacity to contain information than we are at present able to use. Through empowering our mental body we can sharpen our ability to learn faster, and access all information when needed. Our spiritual body is the last and final layer of energy body. All together with the physical body, these are known and referred to as the Five Body System. The Masters, whom I have channeled, use this terminology to refer to the entire spectrum of these energy bodies. Other teachings may have other terminology or may divide the energy bodies differently.

Whatever the system, one fact remains: to return to the bliss and comfort of Oneness, which is our natural state of being, we first need to connect to these energy bodies. The connection is made through the activation of the energy centers or chakras along our physical body. To activate the chakras, we must first clear and cleanse them from the scars, dross and all dense materials we have picked up from many incarnations on Earth. This beloved dark and dense planet which we have called home since we separated ourselves from our true source, is on one hand, the culprit for our misery and on the other hand, our accomplice for the return to Oneness. Somewhere along the way we have somehow tied our fate to that of Earth. The time has come for Earth to release herself from the darkness and the density of matter and we have agreed to be the ones who will facilitate that feat. Over eons of time, there have been many civilizations where souls came to Earth, evolved their species, reached Enlightenment and Ascended by migrating en-mass out of the third dimensional reality. As fate would have it, it has fallen on our civilization to change the course of destiny.

The present race residing on Earth has collectively chosen to bring Enlightenment, not only to our species, but also to Earth; hence all the attention given to the Ascension of Earth. Enlightenment, when looked upon at a planetary scale becomes Ascension. This is what makes us so special and brings the attention of all beings from the four corners of the universe to us. Of course, in this feat, we are supported by the Masters, Great Beings and Cosmic Beings of Light. This is why in Chapter II; Master Jesus gives us a meditational exercise to clear the chakras of the body of Mother Earth, as well as our own.

Archangel Michael comes forth in Chapter III to accelerate us on our path of Enlightenment and Earth's Ascension. He will do so by calling the Pillar of Light to form around us and taking us on a journey to the thirteenth dimension of reality to meet and merge at the Throne of I Am That I Am with the perfected presence of I Am, God in Form.

In Chapter IV Metatron speaks of Ascension for Earth and humankind, and how to facilitate it. He is especially concerned with the well-being of those who are spreading their Light and serving the collective consciousness of humankind and the planet. He offers guidelines to cope with the dense energies coming up to be released both from the masses and the planet. With the release of the dross, the load becomes lighter to facilitate the move from an un-awakened state to a spiritually awakened one. The focus of these energies and the Masters is to return Earth and humankind to a fully awakened state.

We can return to the fully awakened state by moving the energies and the consciousness of Earth and all souls to vibrate at a higher frequency; thereby shifting the focus from the density of this third dimensional realm to a lighter, etheric substance which resembles and replicates the Fourth and Fifth Dimensional Realms. As the saying goes, *"Practice makes perfect."* We shall practice at holding the vibrational frequency at a higher rate and hold space for our newly awakened brothers and sisters on this planet to come to their own. We are here to become the Beacons of Light to remind all souls that we are Divine. The Divine Light runs through us all as individuals, as species and as a planet.

To this end, in Chapter V, Mother Mary offers us, the healers of this world, a cocoon of protection and healing. To be of greatest service to the Earth and humankind, we must first find wholeness within ourselves. The old adage, *"Healer, heal thyself"* is our dire need and dilemma. We are stretching ourselves to do more and this is causing us to burn the candle of our Life Force from both ends. Lord Metatron keeps telling us how deeply in need of healing we are since we have taken such a grave responsibility upon our shoulders.

In Chapter VI, Quan Yin calls upon the three Archangels, Uriel, Raphael and Michael and two personal Guardian Angels, the Angel of Intellect and the Angel of Emotions. The Guardian Angels protect and tend to each individual person's needs. The Archangels are in charge of our collective needs, including the needs of all species and the planet. Quan Yin is also concerned with our mundane needs, therefore in Chapter VII, she offers us a candle grid to promote greater financial abundance and to heal issues relating to personal relationships.

Metatron has introduced many aspects of his own being to us. As prophet Enoch, he has left large bodies of material describing his journey through the Realms of Angels, Archangels, Powers, Principalities, Thrones, Seraphim and Cherubim. The Seven Hierarchies of Angelic Forces above have been given to us by Metatron in various documents which have been called the Books of Enoch, Enoch I and Enoch II. Prophet Enoch is mentioned in the Old Testament of the Bible. Further details of the legend of Enoch and other aspects of Metatron, as the

Archangel, as EI-Shaddai, and as Lesser YHWH can be found in my *Gifts III, Journeys Into the Inner Realms of Consciousness.*

In Chapter VIII, Metatron leads us on an Initiation ceremony to visit with Christ Maitreya and Sanat Kumara. The first, second and third levels of initiation are offered to the students of the Mysteries who have earned the merits to receive them.

In Chapter IX, Master Jesus gives us a meditational exercise to invoke the return of the Lords of Light, the rightful Guardians of Earth. In the meditational exercise, Jesus helps us visualize a Ball of Light growing in the Solar Plexus and emanating Orange Light. This Orange Light helps to increase will power and passion for Life. The Ball becomes a Cocoon and the Cocoon begins emanating Light from our bodies. Then he places the same Ball of Light around the planet and asks us to hold that visualization for Earth. He then beckons us to keep invoking the presence of the Lords of Light to take over the guardianship of Earth.

The Lords of Light are extremely powerful Great Cosmic Beings of Light and could be considered God-parents and the Guardians of the Planet. Their Light is so bright that no darkness or evil can survive in their presence. When they shine their Light upon a planet, peace and harmony ensues. If on the other hand the planet plunges itself into chaos and confusion and allows darkness to seep into its fabric, the Lords of Light withdraw their presence. This is what happened to Earth many thousands of years ago. During the time of Atlantis, our planet was plunged into a sudden state of darkness. According to Universal Law, the Lords of Light had no choice but to withdraw. Fortunately Earth has managed, albeit with great difficulties, to survive in the absence of these Mighty Lords. Over thousands of years, through the help of the Ascended Masters, human beings have been able to pull themselves out of darkness and raise their Quotient of Light. Our Light is now reaching a level, where with some planning and with great willpower, we can demand and decree the return of the Lords of Light. In the meditational exercise, Jesus speaks of the importance of repeating the decrees day and night with all of our power and might, as certain portals of Energy are opened from around October to February each year. These portals are meant to accelerate and to magnify whatever intentions and thoughts are sent to them.

A Portal of Energy is a phenomenon which occurs in the fabric of time and space and acts like a bridge. It extends from the Heavenly Realms to the Earthly Realms. Its purpose is to bring the Heavenly Realms to Earth. Higher Light is induced and focused through these portals in certain receptive locations all around Earth. These locations are vortices of energy. They can be considered entry points or gateways.

These gateways are important because if we raise the energy at those points, we are able to pull a greater vibrational frequency and a greater Quotient of Light through the portal from the Heavenly Realms.

They exist at locations where Higher Light was induced and focused by human beings or the Masters for a reason, at some point throughout history. These focused energies have a time component as well and become even more intense and beneficial at particular points in time. Equinoxes and Solstices are considered important portal dates. The focused time signature moves the energy through these portals with greater focus or intensity. How far down the Light and energy reaches and how much Light we can bring down through the portal depends on our intentions and willpower.

By performing ceremonies at these locations and connecting to these vortices, we can pull in the higher intensity of Light to Earth. These locations are also antennas. They can receive information and transmit it with less interference directly to Earth, magnifying the impact. Seemingly unconscious of the grand plan, many a monument and sacred structure has been built over such vortices through time. The site of Washington Monument, Statue of Liberty, Eifel Tower, Kuala Lumpur Tower, Niagara Falls Tower, Taj Mahal Palace in India and many cathedrals, churches, mosques, temples, and other places of worship are but a few examples. Examples of naturally occurring vortices which bring forth the energy from Portals of Light and magnify the impact are at Victoria Falls, Ayers Rock or Uluru, in Australia, Grand Canyon, Niagara Falls in Canada and U.S.A. The frequency with which the man-made structures seem to fall over such vortices begs the attention of any unbiased bystander and points the finger in the direction of Divine Intervention.

Energy moves through the vortices with greater intensity on portal days. Such dates as 1/1, 2/2, 3/3, and so forth are important energy portal days for each month. New Moon and Full Moon days are also of great importance. The moon acts as a means to recalibrate the energy which comes from the sun. Since energy from the sun originates from the galaxy, the universe and the cosmos beyond, it must be dropped down in intensity. This is the job of the moon. Some people experience sleepless or restless nights during these times. There are other special days during each year where the alignment of the planetary bodies in our solar system creates specific energy exchange. Solar and lunar eclipses are among these.

Performing ceremony on a portal day can bear greater results than on other days. This is why I announce the portal days of each month in a free newsletter on my web site at www.nasrinsafai.com. If you have an intention to set out and you know the location of a vortex of energy, it will be of great benefit to perform a ceremony there on a portal day. When an important energy is coming to Earth, our beloved Masters bring us guidance and direction to perform ceremonies, meditational exercises, invocations and decrees to enhance the anchoring of those energies and to accelerate ourselves on our spiritual and personal path of evolution.

In Chapter X, Metatron continues our journey with another candle grid for Manifestation of Financial Abundance in the short term. In Chapter XI, Master Jeshua brings us to the presence of the World Teacher and teaches us to take a vow of discipleship in his service. Finally, in Chapter XII, Lady Quan Yin, Archangel Michael, Goddess Hecate and Lord Metatron bid farewell to the calendar year. With great love and devotion they offer us advice to take the next step on our journey on the path of Enlightenment.

A GUIDE TO THE CHAKRAS
OF THE PHYSICAL BODY AND THEIR LOCATIONS

Chakras are energy centers that are located upon a central column along the spine. Most traditional thinking refers to seven chakras which are located in the body. In order from lowest to highest, they are: the Root, Sacral Plexus, Solar Plexus, Heart, Throat, Third Eye, and Crown. There are chakras below the Root Chakra which connect us to Earth, and chakras above the Crown Chakra which connect us to the Higher Realms and Heavens above.

Although not traditionally mentioned, there are two other energy centers in the body which the Masters have taught us in our channeling sessions. These are called the Seat of the Soul and the Cosmic Heart. The Seat of the Soul energy center, or chakra, is located halfway between the Heart Chakra and the Solar Plexus, just below the rib cage. The Cosmic Heart Chakra or energy center is located high on your chest, midway between the Heart Chakra and the Throat Chakra. The Cosmic Heart Chakra sits over the thymus gland. We continue to refer to the traditional system of seven chakras and do not allocate a number for the Cosmic Heart and Seat of the Soul Chakras, yet we place equal importance on them.

The chakras of the body above the Crown extend all the way to the thirteenth dimension of reality. The Throne of the I Am That I Am resides in this dimension. The Perfected Presence of the I Am, God in Form, sits upon this Throne. This is considered our Twelfth Chakra.

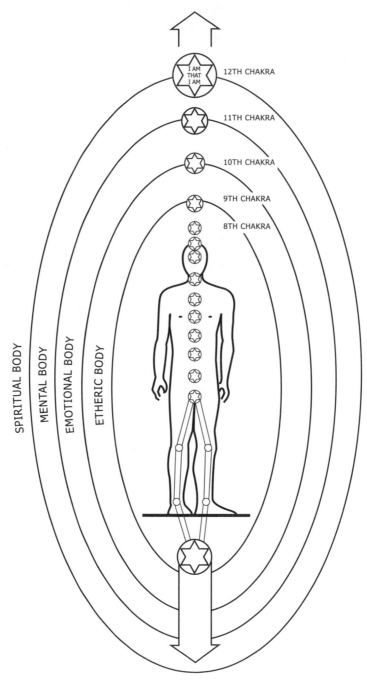

Labels in image: SPIRITUAL BODY, MENTAL BODY, EMOTIONAL BODY, ETHERIC BODY, 12TH CHAKRA (I AM THAT I AM), 11TH CHAKRA, 10TH CHAKRA, 9TH CHAKRA, 8TH CHAKRA

THE FIVE BODY SYSTEM

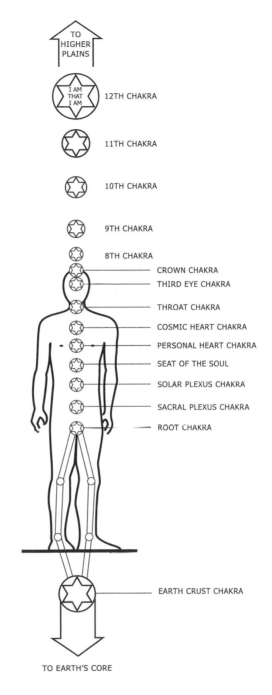

THE CHAKRA SYSTEM

CHAPTER STRUCTURE

Each chapter begins with an introduction given by me, Nasrin. Then the channeled material begins with each Master identifying themselves with their own special style of greeting. For example, Metatron always begins with *"Beloveds of my own heart, I am Metatron, take a deep breath with me"*. Archangel Michael always greets us with *"My Brethren of Light, I am Michael"*, Jesus always begins with, *"Adonai Beloveds, I am Jeshua Ben Joseph,"* and Goddess Hecate and Quan Yin always address us by saying, *"My Children of Light, I am Goddess Hecate or Quan Yin."*

The channeled material also ends when the Master closes withtheir own special signature closing. This usually occurs at the end of each chapter, with the exception of Chapter III, which has three separate channelings.

Please note these important points in order to distinguish between my introduction and the channeled material.

CHAPTER I

INITIATION IN ATLANTIS

We begin the year and the first chapter of this book with a beautiful story told in the sweet energies emanating from our beloved Master Jesus. He comes forth introducing himself with his given name as Jeshua Ben Joseph which is Jesus, son of Joseph. We know him as an Ascended Master. He came to Earth to anchor the energies of Divine Love and was successful in that endeavor. When he left Earth, He became the Master or Chohan of the Sixth Ray, The Ray of Self Sacrifice for the Good of All, or the Ray of Universal Service.

Master Jesus will take us on a journey to Atlantis at a time approximately 30,000 years ago. Atlantis was a large continent whose existence spanned from approximately 250,000 years ago until about 12,000 years ago. The continent of Atlantis was a large land mass in the Atlantic Ocean which included parts of the Eastern and Southern coasts of the United States. The mode of travel was with large vessels that moved on water. Air travel was made possible by vessels that took off from the ships and from land for inter-planetary and galactic travel.

The continent sank somewhere around 12,000 years ago leaving a great rip in the time-space continuum and in the hearts of the Atlantians. Atlantis plays an important role in our present life because the majority of present population of Earth is the returning Atlantians. Many are returning to Earth after a long absence. When rekindled, the memories of the glory of Atlantis and the disaster which lead to its destruction, brings back feelings of both ecstasy and agony.

Many of the souls who have returned to Earth have chosen to shut the memories and hence the abilities to greater inner sight and power. The powers which to us seem extraordinary and supernatural were common place and natural during lifetimes in Atlantis. We begin our journey on the path of Enlightenment with a guided meditational exercise given by Master Jesus. In this exercise, Jesus beckons us to return to Atlantis and retrieve the powers which we held and have since chosen to ignore. The simplest and most necessary exercise on the path of Enlightenment is to open the Third Eye. The Third Eye is a space between the eyebrows on the forehead. This is a center or chakra for communication with the inner realms and a means through which the Masters can communicate with us.

On this meditational journey, we will meet with Sanat Kumara, our Planetary Logos, to receive into our hearts the Divine Flame of Eternal Life. Sanat Kumara is the Father of this planet or the Planetary Logos. In the English dictionary Logos means word of God. I felt this discourse was appropriate for this time of the year; when the energies of Master Jesus and Sanat Kumara are prominent on Earth. This will be a memorable experience and help guide us through the year.

I wish you a great journey into the Light in the presence of our beloved Master Jesus and our Planetary Logos, Sanat Kumara.

Adonai. I am Jeshua Ben Joseph.

At this present juncture in Earth's history, the Masters and Great Beings of Light are deeply engaged in increasing the vibrational frequency of Earth and all humankind. Higher vibrational Light is therefore being brought to Earth to heal Earth and humankind. One of these is an energy which combines the Light of the First Ray of Divine Will with the Fifth Ray of Divine Truth. That means combining the Aquamarine Blue and the Emerald Green Rays together. When mixed, these two create a healing Ray called the Citron Green Ray of Mental Clarity. This energy will be instrumental in clearing the dross from the mental body of Earth and humankind. This cleansing energy is coming directly from the sun. Take a deep breath.

Sanat Kumara

HEALING WITH THE CITRON-GREEN RAY OF MENTAL CLARITY

Visualize this healing Ray showering upon your body. It begins pouring down from the top of your head and moves down your body clearing, cleansing and healing you as it moves down. Visualize that it travels down your torso to your hip, down your legs to the bottom of your feet. The sensation may feel like a shower of Light and energy. Pause for a moment to bathe in these energies and to absorb the healing Light. Take a deep breath.

Feel the sensation of a pulse in the center between your eyebrows at your Third Eye chakra and begin to see the small flicker of a flame.

The flame begins to get bigger until it is about an inch high. You may begin to feel a sensation of warmth or tingling in this area. Continue to hold your focus on the flame. This flame will illuminate the area of your Third Eye and open up your inner visual perception. Once open, it will help you to connect with the inner world to receive direct guidance. Over time, with persistence and continued exercise, you will be fully connected with the Masters directly. As you maintain your focus on your Third Eye, you may feel pressure or discomfort in the area. This is because the flame is facilitating greater opening of this chakra to increase your inner vision. The opening of the Third Eye is an important step toward your evolution on the path of spiritual growth and Enlightenment. The first step to re-establish a connection with the Masters and their realms is by opening and enhancing your inner vision.

You may have resistance in allowing this process to take place. The resistance may be physically experienced as pressure, or headaches. The resistance can be due to fears and pain from experiences in past lives and the fear of being able to see and know more. This may have to do with the events that transpired in certain lifetimes during the time of Atlantis and the pain resulting from the sinking of that land. To release the pressure, you must tell your mind to let go of the fear. Mentally allow yourself to let it go. The pressure will gradually diminish and ultimately release.

The great Generator Crystals imploded leading to the sinking of the land masses directly under them. This alone was a great disappointment and a fearful experience for the inhabitants of that land. The clear quartz crystals were an important and integral part of the Life Force and energy of Planet Earth during the time of Atlantis. They also played an important role in maintaining a high Quotient of Light for the inhabitants of Atlantis.

Some of the available clear quartz crystals are fragments from the original Generator Crystal Clusters. These are found in Brazil. Many pieces are found washed ashore and buried with river rocks. Those who are especially sensitive and remain connected energetically to the events of Atlantis have a special fondness for clear quartz crystal formations. Being in the energy of these crystals can be both healing and helpful in restoring the memories of the events of the time. Merely by touching them, you may feel a current of energy move through you. Sometimes there is the experience of great heat generated by merely touching a piece of these crystal structures. You will therefore benefit from keeping some clear quartz pieces around you when you meditate. The clear quartz can also help accelerate your healing.

At the beginning of the civilization of Atlantis, Sanat Kumara was able to come to Earth every year. He came at the time of each Equinox and Solstice to rekindle the Eternal Flame in the hearts of all humankind by re-igniting the flames at the altars in the Temples of Atlantis all across the continent.

As time went on, density and darkness began to set in. The Light of Earth gradually became dim. Then Sanat Kumara had to remove his energy from Earth, at first gradually and then completely. He finally fully retrieved his energies back to Venus. Some of you were in his service and in his entourage at the time. You made the choice to stay here on Earth. However without his Light and his support, life was exceedingly harsh. The pain of separation and the deep longing to reunite with him, coupled with the harsh state of life on Earth, led to such disappointment that you chose to shut yourself off and forget the connection. Gradually over time as the memories faded and the connection severed, you shut your Third Eye fully and built a few layers of resistance around your heart to protect yourself from further pain and disappointment. Yet the deep longing never ceased. This is why you may feel a yearning even as I recount the story to you and the longing to reunite your energies with him returns. This could be the case with any soul who chose to stay here on Earth. You long to go home, yet you may not even remember where home is, what you are yearning for or who you miss. Take a deep breath.

You may feel a tingling sensation in different parts of your body. This is from the opening of the spiritual energy centers of your body. Energy moves along energetic lines which run throughout your body. There are more than 80,000 points along the energy lines, also known as meridians, where energy moves through the body. Every impulse or tingling sensation is a sign that the healing energy is moving through your body. As the movement of the energy intensifies, it leads to the opening of all your chakras which are important energy centers connecting various layers of your energy bodies to your physical body. This will ultimately lead to bringing the memories of many of your previous lifetimes back to the consciousness of your body. You will recollect the events from many of those lifetimes where your connection with Sanat Kumara and your Soul Lineage has been strong. Connecting with members of your own Soul Lineage and with Sanat Kumara who is the head of that Lineage is like a homecoming. You will re-ignite the memories at your cell structure. Your DNA will be strengthened through the connection with your Soul Lineage members and Sanat Kumara. The memories can awaken in your cell structure and be brought to your conscious recollection.

Your Soul Lineage members are your Soul Family of Light. They are connected to you at a much deeper level than members of your maternal family. Your present family members are with you for this lifetime. Your soul family has been with you since the beginning of time. Once you make this connection, your dreams become more lucid and your meditational journeys more vivid. You may begin to remember the Atlantian temples; the Temples of Wisdom, the Temples of Rejuvenation, Temples of Love, Understanding and Healing. In various lifetimes you have studied there to become the priest or the priestess of these temples.

This was the highest rank. In their advisory role, the priests and priestesses of the temples were the leaders and the rulers over the continent of Atlantis. This was a time when Earth was the scene of interplanetary travel. Let us prepare to take a meditational journey. Take a deep breath.

Meditational Journey to Atlantis

Envision yourself standing in front of Jeshua Ben Joseph. I hold both your hands in the palm of my hands. I hold you close to my own heart to give you greater sustenance. I will take you through the time-space, inside the Pillar of Light.

I call forth the Pillar of Pure White Light of the I Am That I Am. Our destination is The Great Temple of Wisdom in Atlantis. As we move inside the Pillar of Light, our consciousness moves from today's Earth to the Atlantian civilization of 30,000 years ago. We begin to hover over the continent, take note of the design of the city.

Everything is in concentric circles. It is night time. You will see the lights illuminated. The illumination of the light has a golden pink hue.

The main dome of the Temple of Wisdom is at the very center of the inner concentric circle. We will visit this dome. When we reach the entrance you will see a golden gateway. The golden gateway will only open when the emanation from our heart reaches a certain frequency of Light. Those whose level of emanation is lower than necessary will not be allowed to enter. The emanation must be from the heart. Take a deep breath and prepare to enter. The doors open and we enter. We arrive inside the Great Hall. Notice there, a great crystalline structure made of clear quartz. It vibrates a gentle peach pink emanation. We stand before this enormous crystalline structure. Now you will be moved to place the palms of your hands on the flat surface of the crystal. Your head will lean over and you will touch the Crystal with your Third Eye. You will experience an electric charge of energy running through you. The energetic charge will begin emanating from the palms of your hands, your Third Eye and your heart to the Generator Crystal. The Crystal responds by allowing you to penetrate into it. The structure will become fluid and cloud-like and pulls you inside it. You will find yourself inside of the structure and aware that energy is moving through you. You are being recalibrated by the Generator Crystals of the Temple to be brought before the presence of Sanat Kumara. Pause and take a deep breath.

You will walk through the Crystal and find yourself on the opposite side from the one through which you entered. You are standing before a Great Altar. The Altar is circular. Around the Altar the Flame of Eternal Life is burning. The Flame has a pink hue. Take a deep breath.

Stand still and get centered because you will now be in the presence of Sanat Kumara. You will know him as Father. You may find yourself swept by a feeling of loneliness and longing. You are yearning for the loving embrace of a true father and for Divine Love, different from that which is experienced in m ndane realms of physicality in this body of matter. Remembering him will allow you to forget the pain of separation and recall the joy of union. This is a healing gift from the Masters to you. Take a deep breath.

Now visualize the image of Sanat Kumara appearing before you. When you have him fully in your reach, touch the hem of his robes and ask him to give you the Eternal Flame. Ask him to place the Eternal Flame from his own heart into your heart. This is the Eternal Flame of Union between God and humankind. As the Planetary Logos, Sanat Kumara guards and bestows this Flame in the hearts of those who request it. This Flame is the symbol of God-Unity. Visualize yourself standing before Sanat Kumara at the circular Altar. Pink flames are emanating all around the Altar. Sanat Kumara places the fingers of his right hand around his left wrist. With his left hand he reaches into his own Heart Chakra and takes out a Spark. This is the Spark of the Eternal Flame which has been emanating in his heart for many thousands of years. With it, he re-ignites the Flame at the center of the Altar. The entire Altar becomes fully illumined with a deep Fuchsia Pink Light. The flames jump high from the touch of his own Spark. He then takes a Spark from this deep Fuchsia Pink Light and places it inside your Heart Chakra, the Flame warms up your entire chest and brings comfort and peace to you. Take a deep breath.

Visualize Sanat Kumara move to the other side of the Altar where there is a large Throne. He walks to the Throne and sits upon it. Visualize yourself walking behind him. You kneel before him and place your head on his lap. He begins to gently caress your head with his loving hands. Imagine that all your fears, worries and concerns completely disappear. Remember he is the Father who can and will remove your troubles. Feel the warmth from the Eternal Flame in your own heart. Feel it warming your body as you sit calm and relaxed in the presence of Sanat Kumara.

Ask him for whatever you wish to receive from him. Ask for boons and gifts and fulfillment of desires, worldly and spiritual, mundane and sublime, for yourself, for your loved ones, for the planet and all humankind. Ask him to give you guidance. Ask him to make his presence known to you in dreamtime and in wakefulness. Ask him to give you a sign that will help you know when he is around. You may experience an electric sensation in your body. Take a deep breath and pause for a moment to commune with Sanat Kumara.

It is now time to begin to return from this journey. We thank our Lord Sanat Kumara for his love and for all that we have received. We return to stand before the Altar and gratefully bless the Altar. We take our leave. Our return journey will be back through the Generator Crystals which sit at the center of the Great Hall. When you enter into the Generator Crystal, ask to be recalibrated, this time to face the mundane world and maintain your Quotient of Light at a higher vibration. Feel the energy move from the top of your head to the bottom of your feet. You may feel waves of energy moving through your body, causing a sensation of lightness.

Ask for the removal of all energies which no longer serve you. You may feel the release of something from your body. It can be release of dross, forgetfulness, pollution, pain or trauma, loneliness, or abandonment from many lifetimes. Standing at the center inside the crystalline structure, feel yourself showered by Pink Light emanating from the Generator Crystal to restore you to health, wholeness and fill you with love, power, and courage.

We will leave through the golden gateways. Visualize yourself standing close to me as we leave the Temple. We begin to spin through the time space continuum. You might feel nauseous coming back into the consciousness of your body. Take a deep breath.

Remember the presence of Sanat Kumara in these high energy days at the beginning of the year and into the New Year. Ask Archangel Michael to put a Bubble of Light around you, your loved ones, and around your house. Ask that he hold his Sword of Mercy above his head, and over you, your loved ones, and everyone who comes into your house, whether for a visit or to stay. Ask that the same bubble be constructed over the home of your loved ones, wherever they may be.

I offer you golden tulips for this entire year. Tulips are the symbol of spring and the dawning of the New Age. Gold is the symbol for transmutation of dross and return to purity, abundance and prosperity. I offer you a field of golden tulips to bring purity and abundance to enter into the New Golden Age.

Remember to call upon Sanat Kumara everyday from this day on. Remember to visualize the Eternal Flame fully illuminated in your heart. To meditate, call upon me, Jeshua Ben Joseph, hold onto me, let me take you into the Temple of Wisdom; inside of the temple you can contact Sanat Kumara. Repeat this meditation every night; even if it is for a minute or two, you do not have to sit in a long meditation. Right before you fall asleep, visualize yourself going to the Temple of Wisdom with Master Jesus to visit with Sanat Kumara and to re-ignite the Eternal Flame in your heart.

Once the Flame is fully illuminated and anchored in your own heart, you can begin to offer the Flame to all people, places and things. You can ignite the Flame by placing the energy into a flower, into a seed, into the food that you eat, into the air, into the drinking water to energize it. Place your hand around the glass and visualizing the Flame. Wherever you are, you can bless whichever of the Elements you are in contact with. Be aware of the five elements. The five elements are the building blocks of all creation. This entire planet is built by the force of the five elements of Earth, Water, Fire, Air and Ether. Embody and imbue the five elements with the Flame of Eternal Life, and call upon Sanat Kumara. Call him a hundred times a day or more. You can call upon him as Father, Abba. I will be by your side through these auspicious high energy times.

In your love, I am your brother, Jeshua Ben Joseph.

"I offer you a field of Golden Tulips to bring
purity and abundance to enter into the New Golden Age."
Jeshua Ben Joseph

CHAPTER II

CHAKRA OF PHYSICAL BODY AND EARTH

Our beloved Master Jesus, whose given name is Jeshua Ben Joseph (Jesus, son of Joseph), has given us this meditation for the clearing of our own energy body as well as the energy body of Mother Earth. Master Jesus states, *"The clearing which will result from this meditation will impact your bodies in ways that will help you move rapidly in the direction of greater spiritual growth and will help Earth to clear her dross."*

Please continue this meditation for a twenty two day period to complete a cycle of healing. Twenty two is the number for mastery. It is based on the premise that you master anything that you do for a twenty two day period of time. It then becomes part of your being and knowing. It will also be posted on your personal grid and the planetary grid for others to receive and replicate. For each individual, every bit of knowledge, information and wisdom is recorded on a personal grid system which emanates from our body and our auric field, much like a matrix.

The energy of every personal grid, as a species, is posted on the planetary grid. Other members of the species can benefit from the wisdom of all by connecting to each other's grid or by connecting to the overall Planetary Grid. The Guides, Guardians, and Masters use these grids to float new ideas, designs and concepts to all souls. Those souls with greater receptivity retrieve those ideas and use them as tools. Some of these ideas become great new inventions which promote our species to a greater and higher status.

Master Jesus has been greatly involved in the purification process for Earth and all humankind. He has promised many healings and miracles to pave the pathway for the presence of Christ Maitreya, the World Teacher, and the Masters of Wisdom who follow him. When Earth and humankind are purified, the densities prevalent at present can be lifted. With the lifting of density, retrieval of designs and ideas from the Higher Realms becomes easier. We can then accelerate ourselves on the evolutionary path as a species and with our planet and all souls as a whole. In this meditation exercise, Master Jesus teaches us to clear our bodies from pain, density and dross. He also teaches us to do the same on behalf of Planet Earth.

In order to understand the mechanics and be most proficient at this clearing meditation, it is important to understand the energetic make up of our human bodies. For a basic description of the Chakras and the Five Body System, go to the diagram on page 21.

My Beloveds, I am Jeshua Ben Joseph.

Place your focus around your belly. Envision a Ball of Light the size of a large pumpkin turning around your waist. The center of this Ball of Light is located inside your waist about an inch behind your belly button. This is the general area known as the Solar Plexus. It is the center for personal power and control. The natural color of the energy vibrating from the Solar Plexus is Bright Yellow. To energize your Solar Plexus, envision that the pumpkin sized Ball of Light around your waist is emanating a Bright Orange Light. Pause and take three deep breaths as you energize your Solar Plexus with this beautiful Bright Orange Light.

Now visualize that Christ Maitreya, our beloved World Teacher, has come forth to offer you healing Light. He is focusing his healing Light to this general area of your body. Christ Maitreya sends you the energy vibration of Pure White Light. Brilliant Clear White Light covers the entire Ball around your Solar Plexus. The White Light pours into the Ball and changes the color of the Light from Orange to Pure White Light. It then begins to move upward to cover the higher chakras. The energy spins as it moves upward to reach and cover the higher chakras.

The spin is from the left side of the body to the front of the body, to the right side of the body, to behind you and left again (clockwise). It spins first in stationary mode, as if around a central axis. Then it begins to spiral upward like a corkscrew. It will cover the following chakras on its upward path: Solar Plexus, Seat of the Soul, Personal Heart Chakra, Cosmic Heart Chakra (thymus), Throat Chakra, Third Eye Chakra, and Crown Chakra. In each of these chakras you take a deep inhalation, a small pause, and a deep exhalation. You then begin to visualize the energy spinning upward again. Now I will take you through each step of this exercise:

- Visualize Christ Maitreya standing in front of you. He places his hand over your Solar Plexus. The Ball in your Solar Plexus changes colors from a Ball of Orange Light to a Ball of Pure White Light.

- Envision the Ball spinning upward, moving from your Solar Plexus to the next chakra above it. This chakra is called the Seat of the Soul. The center of this chakra is right under your rib cage at the center of your chest where the last two ribs meet. If you touch this area, you may find a tender spot. Push this spot and you will feel the center for the Seat of the Soul Chakra. The Ball of Light spins there. Take a deep inhalation and fill your chest with air; pause for a few seconds; exhale slowly and pause for a few seconds.

- Envision the Ball spinning upward like a corkscrew. While the Ball is in between your chakras, you may take normal breaths. The spin continues, and the energy moves into your Personal Heart Chakra. Take a deep, slow breath in, at your own pace; spinning, pausing. Hold for a second and exhale slow and long.

- Now envision the spin beginning again moving upward to your Cosmic Heart.

- Inhale deep and long; take a small pause, exhale slow and long; the spin begins to move upward. Take a normal breath. Now the spin moves into the throat.

- Inhale, pause, exhale, and begin to spin the energy moving into your third eye. Inhale, pause, exhale, the spin begins to move to your Crown.

This is the process for clearing your own energy centers from Solar Plexus to the Crown and energizing them with the Pure White Light from Christ Maitreya.

Now I will repeat this same exercise and link your energy chakras to that of the Earth's. This time when you begin to spin, visualize the corresponding energy on the chakras of Mother Earth.

- Visualize that you are spinning the Ball of Light in the center of your Solar Plexus. Envision the same Ball of Light spinning in the city of Christchurch, New Zealand, which corresponds to the Solar Plexus of Mother Earth.
- Visualize sending out concentric circles of Light from this point on Earth. The size of Earth's great Ball of Light is the same proportionate size as that of yours. Begin spinning the energy while you focus on this chakra of Mother Earth. Continue to spin, pause, inhale, hold for a second and exhale.
- Visualize moving up to the Seat of the Soul Chakra of Mother Earth. Spin, pause, inhale, hold for a second and exhale.
- Moving up to the Personal Heart Chakra of Mother Earth. Spin, pause, inhale, hold for a second and exhale.

- Moving up to the Cosmic Heart Chakra of Mother Earth. Spin, pause, inhale, hold for a second and exhale.

- Moving up to the Throat Chakra of Mother Earth. Spin, pause, inhale, hold for a second and exhale.

- Moving up to the Third Eye chakra of Mother Earth. Spin, pause, inhale, hold for a second and exhale.

- Finally moving up to the Crown Chakra of Mother Earth. Spin, pause, inhale, hold for a second and exhale.

- At the point when you reach your Crown Chakra and the Crown Chakra of Mother Earth, ask for the Pillar of Light to bring energies from the I Am That I Am.

- The presence of I Am That I Am, God in Form, begins pouring down into your Crown Chakra and that of Mother Earth.

- The purity and innocence that God intended for Earth and humanity is restored both to you and to Mother Earth.

- Envision Pure White Light emanating to you and to Earth.

- Visualize beams of Light, emanating into your Crown Chakra and to the Crown Chakra of Mother Earth at the North Pole.

- The North Pole is bombarded by Pure White Light; your Crown Chakra is bombarded with Pure White Light. This Light emanates and penetrates from your Crown Chakra down your body, as it emanates and penetrates from the North Pole of Mother Earth down to the rest of Earth's body.

- Purity and innocence returns to Earth and to your own body. It moves through you to the bodies of others whom you touch. This exercise will also help in establishing stability for the North Pole to reduce or prevent the impact of natural disasters.

By repeating this exercise, you will serve the Light and bring greater stability and harmony to Earth and all humankind. I support you wholeheartedly in this endeavor.

I hold you in my own heart, Adonai, I am Jeshua Ben Joseph. And so it is.

"When you are able to see the obstacles as a mere distraction
and the distraction an a means to delay you,
then you can see to it that you are neither distracted nor delayed."
Archangel Michael

CHAPTER III

ARCHANGEL MICHAEL'S SWORD

In this chapter you will find three exercises, all of which will empower, accelerate and protect you on the path of spiritual evolution as well as smoothing out your daily lives.

As the Angel of Mercy and Protection, Archangel Michael has offered to come to our rescue and lighten up our load from the dross and the darkness of the mundane realm of physicality. Archangel Michael introduces us to the Pillar of Pure White Light. This is a great gift. When we call forth the Pillar of Pure White Light, we can raise our vibrational frequency and put the protection inherent in this Light all around us. Archangel Michael then brings us the activation of our Swords of Mercy to add further protection and Higher Light. A Light Grid meditation channeled through Quan Yin is given to enhance the activation of the Sword of Mercy by Archangel Michael by invoking the presence of the Goddess energies of Lady Faith, Goddess Hecate and Quan Yin. Quan Yin was the Guardian of the Violet Flame of Transmutation for over 14,000 years until she passed the guardianship of the Flame onto St. Germain. At this present moment we have entered the Age of Aquarius which is the entry point into the Seventh Golden Age signaling the dawning of 1,000 years of peace.

In March we celebrate the Equinox which falls somewhere between the 19th and 22nd of the month according to the time zone you are in and the lunar configuration. The three days around the Equinox are energy days of great importance. Energies pour in the day before, the day of and the day after the point at which the sun moves into the equator at Equinox. At each Equinox and Solstice, heightened energies are sent to our planet to help us manifest our Divine Mission and accelerate our spiritual growth. This is the time to ask and to offer everything to the Divine Will. Every morning, start your day by calling upon the presence of the I Am That I Am, your favorite Ascended Masters and Divine Mother and say, "I am the embodiment of your Divine Will today." End the day by invoking the presence of the Pure White Light from Source and say, *"I am the embodiment of your Divine Will tonight."*

I wish you a great journey of acceleration on your path of Light at this prime time. These are times of accelerated manifestation of our thoughts. Therefore, be careful about what you think; good, bad, and indifferent, they all count! Let us therefore plan to focus upon positive and productive ways to accelerate ourselves on our path to attain greater Light.

RAISING YOUR VIBRATION THROUGH THE PILLAR OF PURE WHITE LIGHT. MERGING WITH THE I AM PRESENCE AT THE THRONE OF THE I AM THAT I AM.

My Brethren of Light, I Am Michael.

As you traverse on the path to Enlightenment, you may find that hardships and obstacles are placed on your path to test you. This will make you stronger and bring you wisdom. When you pass these tests, you evolve further. The obstacles are like rotten eggs. The fear of facing the obstacle is like the smell of a rotten egg. You can get rid of the smell when you get rid of the egg. The anticipation of how and what you do, the fear and anxiety of facing the obstacle brings you down and lowers your Light. Problems and obstacles serve by distracting humankind from the Light. Yet, through the distractions, they make you stronger. By your efforts to remove them, you gain momentum and become more determined to pursue Light. The more Light you hold, the greater your ability to cope with future distractions and obstacles. As you evolve spiritually, you become worthy of greater Light and with it comes the ability to conquer all obstacles.

When you are able to see the obstacle as a mere distraction and the distraction as a means to delay you, then you can see to it that you are neither distracted nor delayed. To achieve this task, I will teach you to call the Pillar of Pure White Light to form around you. The purpose of this pillar is to raise your vibrational frequency to help you feel connected to the Source. Then, you are not easily distracted or affected by problems and obstacles. Obstacles can only have an adverse impact on you when you allow them to. You allow them to have such an impact because you feel lonely, left out, fearful and at a loss to cope.

When the Pillar is fully formed and you reside inside of it permanently, you can remain detached from the fear of failure and the feeling of loneliness, separation and rejection. When you are inside the Pillar of Light, you connect to the Perfected Presence of the I Am That I Am, God in Form. This is the individualized presence of God which has taken form and resides at the thirteenth dimension of reality. Through your Twelfth Chakra you are able to connect with this dimension and experience the perfected presence of the I Am That I Am, by merging and uniting with the presence.

This is perhaps the most important step in returning to the perfection of our Original Divine Plan. The Divine Plan as originally intended by God was to allow you to remain connected to God and to the Pure White Light at all times and in all circumstances. Once connected, there could be no fear of separation or loneliness. The Perfected Presence of the I Am That I Am, also known as the I Am Presence or simply the I Am, is also called the Magical, Luminous, Glorious, Victorious Presence.

To change the energy in you and around you and to raise your own vibration to Higher Light; every morning as you arise, call upon the Pillar of Pure White Light to form around you. Enter into the Light and move to unite with the Presence of the I Am. Do this again at night before you fall asleep.

MEDITATION TO RECEIVE AND HOLD PURE LIGHT AND UNITE WITH THE I AM PRESENCE

I now offer you a procedure to raise your vibration to Higher Light and to stay protected in the Pure White Light of the I Am at all times. Now take a deep breath and sit or lay down in a comfortable position to begin this meditational exercise.

Say this invocation,

> *"I call upon the Pillar of Pure White Light to descend upon me and to form around me. I call upon the Presence of the I Am That I Am. I ask the Presence of the I Am That I Am to join and merge with me."*

You may have difficulty feeling a change or a shift in your own energy field at first. It is important that you persevere and continue to ask for the Pillar of Light to surround you. Sometimes your vibration has become so slow that the Presence of the I Am That I Am cannot reach you. This is because there is a certain level of energy vibration below which it will not extend. Therefore, you will have to raise your own vibration to a frequency which will reach up to the Presence. The Pillar of Light will raise the vibration around you. As you stand inside of it, the lower vibrations dissolve and you begin to gather more Light and Energy.

Ask for the Pillar of Light, Cylinder of Light, Tunnel of Light; it matters not how you say it; what is important is to surround yourself in Light and allow it to heighten your vibration. Visualize the Presence waiting for you at the top of this Pillar, Cylinder or Tunnel. Imagine it to be there. Let your heart convince your mind that it is there. At that point, begin to move the energy upward through your Crown Chakra at the top of your head.

50

Move up inside this Pillar of Light in the direction of Higher Light. There are chakras above your head (chakras eight through twelve). Visualize that the energy moves up to your Eighth Chakra. Pause to energize that chakra and move up to the Ninth, Tenth, Eleventh and Twelfth Chakras. Pause and take a deep breath at each chakra.

Energy reaches the Twelfth Chakra in the thirteenth dimension of reality. This is the Throne of the I Am That I Am. You shall meet with the Presence of the I Am, who is the essence of God manifested in form, seated at the Throne of I Am That I Am.

Now visualize yourself approaching to meet the Presence of the I Am. Pause to merge and unite with the Presence. The Presence has an Ethereal Body emanating Pure Light, shimmering emanating from every direction. Pause and meditate for a while as you bathe in the energy of the I Am Presence.

Each time you practice this meditation, you will be able to absorb a higher level of Light, until you can begin to imbue and embody the Light of the Presence of the I Am That I Am. Then you may be invited to sit upon the Throne of the I Am That I Am and fully absorb the Light. Once you are fully merged, request the Presence to come down with you into your body. Do this for three rounds.

> *Round 1:* Meet, merge and unite with the I Am Presence. Bring back and imbue your body with the Presence from the top of your head to the bottom of your feet, and further to the core of Mother Earth.
>
> *Round 2:* Move up again inside the Pillar of White Light to the Presence of the I Am That I Am; mixing, merging

and uniting in Oneness. Pull that energy vibration down and bring it into every chakra of your body and being, down to the bottom of your feet and from your feet into the core of Mother Earth.

Round 3: Go back up the same way, and after you have merged with the I Am Presence, ask your questions and offer your prayers. Sit for a moment and listen. Answers come when they are needed. To replenish yourself, bring the united and merged essence of the I Am That I Am down into your body to stay with you from this moment on.

Practical uses for this exercise:

When you are in the middle of a meeting, a group conversation, with a client, a patient, a family member or a child and you feel as though your words are not penetrating, or you are losing your focus, excuse yourself for a moment to compose yourself. Go to the restroom, if that is the only way you can have privacy. Have a precious moment of Oneness to regroup and practice the above exercises. It will take you a few minutes at first to go through the steps. It may take a while for you to feel the impact. As you practice and become familiar with the steps, you will feel the change faster. You can reach a place where the impact becomes instantaneous.

To return to Oneness and free yourself from the separation, you must first merge and unite with that aspect of God which has form, the Presence of the I Am That I Am. The Luminous Presence of God in form may appear to you like a human being. It may seem androgynous, or appear as male or female. That is your personal, individual experience.

If you do not actually see the being, you may get flashes of Light or sensations in your body of calmness and peace. You may feel a warm, fuzzy feeling as though you have come back to a loving home.

The Presence of the I Am That I Am is your Divine Right. The Presence of the I Am That I Am holds the essence of Oneness. You will return to the I Am in order to know and remember this Oneness. The journey of God-Unity and the Ultimate attainment of Enlightenment is through this Presence.

In the Luminous Presence of the I Am, I am your brother Michael. So it is.

ACTIVATION AND RECALIBRATION OF THE SWORD OF MERCY

My Brethren of Light, I am Michael.

Feel the presence of your own brother, Michael the Archangel, Guardian of Protection, standing before you. Mika-El is a name given to me that literally means *"as is God"* or *"in the likeness of God."* Mika-El is the Guardian Angel instructed by God to protect and guard humankind against all harm.

Cocoon of Aquamarine Blue Light of Protection

As I stand before you, I will begin to emanate an Aquamarine Blue Light from my heart to your heart and from my auric field to your auric field. Visualize beams of Light pouring out of my heart to your heart. Emanations of Aquamarine Blue Light which permeate in my aura begin to fill your auric field and encapsulate you. The Aquamarine Blue Light emanating from my body is the same blue color that you see around the flame on a gas stove. That Blue Light begins to emanate from your body as well. Focus on receiving this Blue Light and allow it to enter into your body. It begins to gather and accumulate in the space of your Heart Chakra. Then visualize it extending from your Heart Chakra to all parts of your body. Finally reaching out to the surface of your skin, it begins to pour out into your auric field. It then expands to the edges of your auric field to create an Aquamarine Blue Cocoon around you.

This Cocoon of Light will protect you from all harm and heal you from all ailments. Allow the energy, as it moves through your body, to bring peace and comfort to your body, your mind, your emotions and your soul. Ask that the consciousness of your body be receptive to this healing Light.

Say, *"In the name of the I Am That I Am, I call forth the presence of Archangel Michael to instill the Aquamarine Blue Light of Protection within me and around me. I command my consciousness and all my personality aspects to receive, absorb, emit and to be healed by this Aquamarine Blue Light of Divine Mercy."*

Pause for a moment while you are absorbing these energies. Take a few deep breaths.

Activation of the Sword of Mercy

To activate and recalibrate your Sword of Mercy, I call your Higher Self and all aspects of your personality to come forth. I hold my Sword of Mercy drawn out of its sheath to activate your Sword of Mercy. Every individual who is physically incarnate has such a sword; however, it may be dormant. Even though I call it a sword, in essence, it is a column of Light that sits on top of your spinal column. When activated, it emits the same Aquamarine Blue Light which emanates from my Sword.

Some people are born with their column of Light fully illuminated and active. These remember their divinity and have a special affinity with me. At some point in your spiritual evolution, you reach the phase where the Sword of Mercy must be reactivated, as a reminder of your own Divine Heritage and a means to reconnect you with your Source.

Every soul has originated from the same Light held within the heart of God, the Undifferentiated Source, or God in Non-manifest Form. Therefore every soul is entitled to recall their Divine Heritage back to them. All souls are pieces of the One Great Soul. God as Undifferentiated Source chose to take form and to manifest as many souls. Therefore, all souls belong to the same original Source, and are entitled to return to their Divine Origin. The activation of your Sword of Mercy will help you recall your Divine Origin and assist you to return to that divinity.

I lift my Sword of Mercy to re-activate your Divine Energies in you by holding it upright in front of you. This will accelerate you on your journey to the Divine Source.

This exercise will recalibrate the active Sword of Mercy to harmonize its energies with the level of spiritual attainment at this present phase of your life. It will continue to recalibrate you as you move to higher attainments. The exercise of recalibration would be relevant to your spiritual status and your spiritual level of elevation. The Sword maintains its own consciousness; it is connected directly with the energies of Mika-El, (Michael) the Guardian Angel of Mercy and Protection.

Take a deep breath and focus your attention on your body. Visualize that Archangel Michael is now pointing his Sword of Mercy at your body. A column of Aquamarine Blue Light begins to emanate from the base of your spine to the top of your head. The color ranges from a light Aquamarine Blue to a medium Cobalt Blue. This Blue Column is filled with the Flame of Divine Mercy. The Ray and the Flame are Feminine and Masculine polarities of the same energy vibration. The Ray represents the Feminine Aspect and has a gentle Feminine Liquid Light vibration. The Flame has a fiery Masculine and active vibration.

As the activation begins, you may feel a sensation which can be heat, coolness, tingling or a wave of energy moving up and down your spine. At the top of your head you may experience pressure as if energy is moving upward and outward. At the base of your spine you may feel the energy moving down and out. The Sword of Mercy, which has been sitting dormant along your spinal column, is now activated. Its activation will cause the movement of energy up and down your spinal column.

Once the activation is complete, you will be able to use your own Sword of Mercy as a tool for protection and for unification with Archangel Michael and the Legions of Michael. Those of you who have always felt an affinity and kinship with Archangel Michael and his Legions, may be eager to reinforce this connection through the activation and recalibration of your own Sword.

Pause for a moment, close your eyes and visualize the Sword of Mercy activated along your spinal column. Visualize a column of Aquamarine Blue Light emanating along your spinal column. It covers from approximately five inches below your tail bone, along your spinal column, to five inches above your head, over your Crown Chakra. Feel the Aquamarine Blue Light of Divine Will. The Masculine and the Feminine energies held within the Ray and the Flame are now moving along your spinal column. Imagine that you settle energetically into a peace and stillness which results from this activation. Be still and feel it vibrating throughout your body. The energies of the activation and recalibration of your Sword of Mercy reach a deep stillness in the core of your being.

For best results, try to repeat this exercise for twenty two consecutive days. Every day call for the presence of Archangel Michael by your side and reinforce this exercise throughout the day. Invoke his presence every night asking for a recalibration of your Sword of Mercy. Twenty two is the number for mastery. You can master whatever you focus upon by repeating it twenty two times. At the end of this, the activation and recalibration will be fully established within you. Then you only need to re-energize your Sword through this full meditation occasionally.

You may choose to repeat this exercise at the time of Spring and Fall Equinox and at Summer and Winter Solstice. This will give you elevation and acceleration of your spiritual growth. Repeat this exercise whenever you feel the need for an extra boost and closeness with Archangel Michael.

In the love of the Undifferentiated Source, I am your brother, Michael.

QUAN YIN'S GRID TO REINFORCE THE SWORD OF MERCY WITH THE ENERGIES OF TRANSMUTATION, POWER AND LIFE FORCE

My Children of Light, I am Quan Yin.

I invite Archangel Michael to come forth and to reactivate and recalibrate the Sword of Mercy that illuminates your body and Life Force. This Sword of Mercy is a symbol of Archangel Michael and the Angelic Legions of Mercy. It sits upon your spinal column. It extends five to ten inches above the top of your head and five to ten inches below your tailbone. It vibrates a deep Aquamarine Blue color, especially in moments where you prepare for sending Healing Light, and in deep meditation. The energy vibrates flashes of Blue Light. When a healing takes place, the Blue Light is transmitted from the healer into the bodies and beings of those who are to be healed and the atmosphere around them. When this Light is active inside of your body, it emanates Divine Love. The activation of the Sword brings healing to your body and your being. You can send it out to all beings, people, plants, animals and the five elements: Earth, Water, Fire, Air, and Ether. In times of need your innate senses know how to heal you through energizing your body with the Blue Light.

I call upon our Lord Archangel Michael and his consort Lady Faith to come forth and I call upon the Legions of Lord Michael and Lady Faith to take their position around your body, creating a circle of Light. I ask Lord Michael to stand in front of you, pointing his Sword of Blue Flame at your heart and Lady Faith to stand behind you, pointing her Sword of Blue Flame at the back of your heart. I ask the presence of our beloved Goddess Hecate to take her position with her Sword of Mercy to your left. Quan Yin will hold the Sword of the Blue Flame intertwined with the Flame of the Violet Flame of Transmutation and will stand to your right. The Violet Flame is a fifth dimensional energy which transmutes all negative and lower vibrational frequencies into Light.

I ask Goddess Hecate to intertwine her Sword of Power with her Sword of Red Flame of Life Force from Mother Earth. Hecate is given Divine Power to hold the leash upon all the Dark Forces. I ask that she point her Sword at your left shoulder as I point my Sword of Blue and Violet Flame at your right shoulder. We begin to transmit the Energies of Transmutation, Power, Life Force and Mercy. Archangel Michael and Lady Faith will begin to transmit the Blue Flame of Protection and Mercy.

You may feel a tingling sensation or heat moving up and down your body. You may see this Blue Light flashing; sparkles of Light may begin flashing before your inner vision. At some point in this process, as the Red, Violet and Blue Light begin to intermingle with one another, there will be an explosion of Light in your Heart Chakra. At that moment this energy will become part of your own essence and you will be recalibrated to greater Light. The Sword of Mercy will remain activated from this day on. Do this exercise for twenty two days and allow your energy body to accept the vibration of the Sword of Mercy as part of its own beingness. In gratitude to Michael and his Legions, Faith and her Legions, and Goddess Hecate,

I am your Mother, Quan Yin.

"I now call the 24th of April of each year the Ascension Day...
Ascension Day for Earth, Ascension Day for humanity.
The 24th of April of every year will be considered
Ascension Day from the Ascended Masters' point of view."
Metatron

CHAPTER IV

ASCENSION DAY AND PARAMATMAN

In this discourse Metatron speaks of the Energies of Ascension. Metatron tells us how to stand in Truth and dissolve negative emotions and promote healing, awakening and transformation of ourselves and the planet. To that end, He then goes on to teach us how to prepare our bodies, emotions, mind, soul and spirit for elevation to higher vibrations of Light. For deep clearing and cleansing of the body and being, Metatron gives directions on cleansing the body with salt and lavender baths, mantras to repeat, breathing exercises and construction of an etheric candle altar, inside the palace of your own heart.

Beloveds of my own heart, I am Metatron. Take a deep breath with me.

The greatest way for the Truth to come to the surface is to send love. When someone has been untrue to you, they are sending the darkness of untruth around them. If you react to that untruth, you are adding to it. If you hold the Light, and send love and Light to that untruth, what happens? That love surrounds the untruth and the untruth will have to begin to fold upon itself. As it folds upon itself, it is engulfed with your love and your Light. Shrinking and shriveling into smaller portions until, ultimately, the untruth will have to fold completely upon itself, becoming a point of darkness and give way to the Light, dissolving completely into the Light.

You can do this with any negative emotion whether it is untruth, greed, deception, betrayal or fear — and fear is the mother of all negative emotions. Every negative emotion has its roots in some type of fear. It may be fear of loss, fear of darkness, fear of not having enough or fear of death. Fear turned within becomes anger, anger turned within becomes rage, and rage when it is suppressed deeply becomes depression. All fears stem from darkness. When you send Light to surround it, it shrinks and shrivels and ultimately releases itself into the Light. When it does, there is no fear and no negative emotion. What then remains is peace and harmony, union and goodness. That goodness will lead you to the Light of the I Am That I Am, the Light of God in Form. When you reach to the Light of the I Am, you begin to heal all your fears and let go of the sense of separation. Your individual self unites with the Higher Self in the essence of the I Am That I Am.

Healing, awakening and transformation begin at the individual level and will gradually spread to the consciousness of the masses at the planetary level. The ripple of the individual effect moves from one to the next, and goes around the globe to reach every soul.

As human consciousness begins embracing the Higher Self, all incarnate souls on the planet, including the five elements, will follow suit. This is because human beings have taken the responsibility for being the consciousness of the planet. The decision-making acts for the entire planet and all souls are entrusted to them.

Therefore, once human beings make the decision to move from the lower self to the Higher Self, all of the elements which are the building blocks of the planet itself will also make that decision and move from the lower self to the Higher Self. Then the waters of Earth will automatically release the pollution, the air will automatically release the pollution, the greenhouse effect will no longer impact Earth and the melting of the mountain snowcaps and icebergs will stop.

The Five Elements *(Earth, Air, Fire, Water, Ether)* have their own consciousness which has always been aligned with the Divine Consciousness. Their alignment has been lost because the human consciousness has fallen. The lower consciousness has led mankind to acts of unconscious behavior which tampers with and misaligns the forces of nature and the five elements. It is the legacy of humankind to be the guardians and caretakers of Earth and all forces of nature, including the five elements. The moment that the human factor turns around and embraces its own legacy, its own Divine Light, its own Divine Purpose, then all the elements will return to their Divine Purpose.

The great plan to be accomplished by 2012, is the alignment of the small self of every human being with the Great Self in the Presence of the I Am That I Am (or complete merging of the I Am, the Great Self into the body). There will be no more distinction between the lower self and the Higher Self. There will be no more distinction between the small I and the great I. The I Am resides within the being and the body of every human being.

I now call the 24th of April of each year the Ascension Day; Ascension Day for Earth, and Ascension Day for Humanity. The 24th of April of every year will be considered Ascension Day from the Ascended Masters' point of view. What do I mean by the Ascension Day?

The Feminine Principle of Existence is descending upon humanity. The Presence of the I Am is descending upon humanity; entering into the body of matter, materializing spirit and entering into the world of physically manifest energy vibration. This is an important turning point for all humanity. It represents another step in the process of materializing spirit; opening the heart, realizing the True Self (Atman), and aligning the True Self with the Supreme Self (Paramatman).

The 24th of April is a day when the Supreme Self will open up its heart to be received by the self of all souls, the self of the planet, the self of the solar system, the self of the galaxy, the five elements, the hearts of all people, places and things, and the heart of all souls.

The 24th of April is the day that the spirit of the I Am moves through the soul of all things. The year 2005 set the pace for the next 1,000 years and obviously beyond. Why is it obvious? Because the year 2005 was the entry point of the 1,000 Years of Peace. Whatever the nature of this peace is going to be from the very beginning, it sets the pace for the next 1,000 years. And whatever the pace of that 1,000 years becomes, that sets the pace for the following thousands of years. This is why I stress the importance of these days.

Wherever you are on the 24th of April each year, it is a day of celebration, remembrance, reflection, contemplation, prayer and vigilance. We are now preparing for the completion of the 1,000 years of peace by, every day, encouraging the Paramatman Light, the Supreme Self, to enter in the space of the heart. We also prepare by encouraging the I Am Presence, the True Self, to enter into our body and beingness. This begins materializing the spirit of the Oneness in the body and beingness of all things.

To prepare for the higher energies, we will cleanse the body, clear the emotions, still the mind and purify the soul. We invite the entry of the soul into the physical body. We desire, intend, and will to cleanse the body of matter to receive the essence of the soul and anchor the True Self within our beingness. This is the description of a soulful person; when the body and beingness is brimming with the brilliance of the soul; when the soul is over-lighting the body, extending and illuminating itself in the body and beingness of a human being. That makes a human being soulful.

The important point is, how can one touch that soulfulness and maintain the presence of the soul within the body and being, not for a moment, not for an hour, not for one performance but for an entire lifetime and beyond? How can one merge into the presence of the soul and remain vibrant in that soulfulness and not lose it over time. How can we invoke and invite the soul to enter permanently? How? With a great loving heart, with great perseverance, with great patience and with acceptance, it will happen; soulfully, patiently and gradually. It will happen in steps. The first step is that you hold onto the soul as you fill your beingness with that higher vibration for a moment. Then you extend that moment for an hour. Then you have a few of these hours of soulfulness throughout the day. Then the edges of these hours touch, and it becomes a wave that ebbs and flows until finally it flows continuously without stopping. It emerges from the Paramatman Light; the source of the Highest Light, the source of the Supreme Self. It illuminates the human self, first for a moment, then for a few moments, and finally for eternal moments of communion in the body. You materialize spirit in the body and illuminate the body with spirit.

When the soul enters, that is the indication that the spirit is arriving. Soul is the vehicle; spirit is the breath. When you fully prepare the vehicle, the breath will come, whether that vehicle is your own body, a blade of grass, Mother Earth, a mustard seed, or the cosmic conglomerate.

Physical Body: Intentional Breath

What should we do for the physical body? Let us begin from the zero point. Lighten up the body. Breathe. In the same way that you eat three times a day, make it a habit to exercise deep breathing for five minutes before each meal. If you do not remember before the meal is over, then give yourself a five minute deep breathing time at the end of the meal. If you still forget, then do the exercise as soon as you remember.

How should one breathe? Take four deep breaths so deep that you can feel it from the base of your spine to the top of your shoulders. One breath cycle should be a long, deep inhalation followed by a long, slow exhalation. Repeat this cycle for about five minutes. As each day goes by, you will see that you can extend the breath a little bit longer increasingly each day. The first few days you may start seeing flashes on the horizon of the TV screen behind your closed eyes. This is because you are oxygenating your body and the energy moves in the head and that is perfect. Gradually the long, deep breaths, inhaling and exhaling, will fill you with Light.

Mantra for Intentional Breath

With each inhalation say,

"I Am the Paramatman Light. I breathe the Paramatman Light."

With each exhalation say,

"I become the Paramatman Light. I Am the Paramatman Light."

Or you can say all four lines together for each inhalation and all four lines for each exhalation, if you are able to breathe for that length of time in and out.

With the first deep breath, say the mantra and enter into full inhalation. Then begin a slow, rhythmic exhalation. Purse your lips with the exhale as though you are about to whistle, and let the air move slowly and gently through your slightly open mouth, as if you want to push the breath out, but your lips are holding a very small portal for its exit. Follow with the second, third and the fourth deep breaths.

Follow the four deep breaths with three normal breaths, whatever a normal breath is for you, in order to prepare for the entry of the Presence of the Paramatman into your body. As you practice this exercise daily, your breathing rhythm changes. A normal breath at the very beginning may become a different kind of breath than after thirty days of exercise. The normal breath itself can become a soft, smooth, long breath, if you do the exercise properly. The normal breaths are meant to bring focus back to the body. The deep breaths are meant for the Paramatman Light to enter into the body and to awaken the body to the entry of the soul. The normal breaths are to adjust to that awakening. The focus is to remind the self, the body, the mind and the emotions that this important event is on-going.

Physical Body: Exercise

Every movement of the body is good, such as stretching, tapping, jumping, jogging, or running, as long as it expands the body. Awaken the physical body in whichever way is appropriate for you. Runners may have to run the same mile slightly faster to be reminded that the exercise is to make way for the re-entry of Paramatman Light. A sedentary person may have to take a leisurely walk to be reminded of the same truth. Everyone must allow the physical body to exercise itself as a reminder of the re-entry of Paramatman Light. A few minutes of breathing is for meditation and reflection; a few minutes of physical exercise is for opening the gateways of the body to receive the Paramatman Light.

Physical Body: Food Intake

Think of this month as a cleansing month and eat light foods. If you could become a fruitarian in an instant, I would recommend it during this month. However, for most of us, this could be detrimental. Your body has become toxic from eating different types of foods. Going from full range of foods to only fruit will bring the toxicity to the surface and will make you sick. If you are 100% vegetarian, make fruits a larger percentage of your food intake. If you are a 100% meat and cooked food eater with hardly any raw vegetables, juices or fruits, then begin with 1% progressing towards 10%, 15%, 20%. Make it your intention to continue in that direction with 1% increments, and gradually increase the percentage of raw foods in your diet. If you are used to eating three solid meals of cooked food that is bulky in nature such as hamburger, fries and a soda for lunch, then think of the possibility of incorporating an item of fruit and gradually increase that amount to replace some part of that meal. If you are skipping the bread around the hamburger, a salad or an apple can replace it. Gradually if you always eat a salad with some chicken then have that salad with a few nuts instead of the chicken. Or reduce the amount of chicken and increase the intake of raw fruit, vegetable, or nut protein, bearing in mind that nuts are acidic in nature (too much acid brings imbalance to the body causing illness).

I am not asking you to make dramatic changes which your body can not cope with. Make changes which your body will allow you to make without crisis. I am also asking you that if the crisis starts to build up, do not be afraid. If after one week of doing well your body suddenly craves a hamburger, and you fixate on the idea until your mind becomes incapacitated, then by all means, eat a hamburger. Let it sit on your stomach and wreak havoc. Then your mind can let go of the idea of the hamburger. As the energies become lighter, lighter food becomes more palatable.

Physical and Auric Body: Bathing with Salt and Lavender

Next on the agenda is the bathing of the body. Every third day take a salt bath or shower. Preferably do this at night before you go to sleep. Use Epsom salt, sea salt, mineral salt or rock salt; failing all of that, use kitchen salt. A spoonful of kitchen salt can do wonders for your body if no other choices are available.

If you prefer to take showers, take a liter jug (size can be approximate) with a tablespoon of salt into the shower with you, fill it with warm water and shake it. At the end of your shower, turn the shower off then fully douse yourself from the top of your head to the bottom of your feet with the salt water. Leave the salt on your body. The salt cleanses all the dross and impurities from your body. Next fill the jug again and add six drops of lavender oil to the jug of water. Douse yourself by pouring it from the top of your head to the bottom of your feet. Walk out of the shower with the lavender sitting on top of every pore of your body. Every breath that your skin takes is taken through the cocoon of the lavender. Do not vigorously rub the towel on your body. Be aware that you are dripping with lavender oil. Tap yourself dry gently. Go to bed with the lavender in your auric field. Lavender brings calmness to your auric field and induces peaceful sleep.

If you take baths, add the salt into your bath water. The salt will completely clear your body of impurities; these are energies that are released from your body, the body of Mother Earth and other human beings. Drain the tub and douse yourself with the lavender oil in the jug of water as mentioned above. Then pat yourself dry. When you take the salt bath or shower, make sure the palms of your hands, the tips of your fingers and the bottom of your feet are doused in the salt water as well as the lavender water. You can put your hands fully in the jug. If the jug has a tight bottleneck, then just pour the water mixture on the palms of your hands, and then rub your hands together to the tips of your fingers. Then lift up each foot and gently pour some water mixture on the bottom of your feet, all the way to the tips of your toes and the soles of your feet. Do this with both the salt and the lavender.

Mental and Emotional Body Healing

Here is an exercise for the healing of your mental and emotional body. Catch your mind when it begins to belabor a point which leads to fear, worry, concern, anger or any other negative thought or emotion.

Stop and say the mantra. Breathe deeply and repeat,

"I Am the Paramatman Light.
I breathe the Paramatman Light.
I become the Paramatman Light.
I Am the Paramatman Light."

For your emotional body clearing, when you find yourself deeply engrossed in the highs and lows of emotional influences, stop. Take a deep breath and offer that emotion up for clearing by saying the mantra,

"I Am the Paramatman Light.
I breathe the Paramatman Light.
I become the Paramatman Light.
I Am the Paramatman Light."

To clear your mind, think less! Become the observer. To clear your emotions, watch the highs and lows of your emotions and do not participate in those fluctuations. Watch the thoughts of emotions ebb and flow, and get out of the flow. Snap out of it. When you harness an emotion, you simply jump out of the emotion, and it has no hold over you. You go back to being in control. Better still, you never lose your control or give in to the highs and lows of emotions. You are in control of that emotion; that emotion is no longer in control of you. Within the individual self and within groups, conflict arises when emotions take the upper hand among the group members. Even wars are fought when emotions take control.

Spiritual Body Cleansing

Light a candle for your spiritual body cleansing, preferably at night for a few minutes before you go to sleep. During the first two weeks, light a white candle for the return of purity and innocence. During the second two weeks, light a deep purple candle for the transmutation of all dross and duality. Light the candle after you have taken your salt and lavender bath at night. Do the breathing exercises at the last few minutes of your meditation.

Plan to light the candle for one month from whenever you start. It does not matter when you begin during the course of the month or how it relates to the 24th of April. Even if you start these exercises in the middle of September, October or November it will work wonders.

Summary

The components of this exercise are to perform:

1. Breathing exercises

2. Repetition of the mantra

3. Physical body clearing

Eat raw fruits and vegetables, incorporating their energy vibration into the body. Start from 1% raw food and move toward 100% in your final fruit and vegetable diet. To clear the energy in your environment, burn candles; white for two weeks, purple for two weeks. To clear the energy of your body, use the salt bath or shower followed by dousing yourself in lavender oil.

In these exercises we have physical body clearing, emotional and mental body clearing, auric body clearing and spiritual body clearing. The mantra and the breathing clear the body for the spirit to enter. All of this together is the process of materializing spirit. We are materializing spirit to bring Ascension to your body and your beingness. Through each individual human being, Ascension can be brought to Earth.

All of these exercises will continue to be valid at any point in the year for your evolution and elevation to greater Light.

Mobile Candle Altar

For those of you who are unable to make an actual candle altar or when a stationary altar is not practical, you can start by visualizing the candle grid in your heart. Begin right here, right now. Visualize in the space of your heart the white candle burning to bring the original state of purity and innocence back to your body. After two weeks, visualize a deep purple candle burning for the transmutation of all dross. Ask that this candle grid be illuminated at all times. You will hold a mobile candle grid within your heart with your intentions, wherever you go. Take a deep breath.

Phase I: Energizing with the White Light of Purity and Innocence: Spiritizing Matter

Envision yourself inside the palace of the heart where an altar has been prepared. On that altar we will place a tall, very tall, white pillar candle which will burn nonstop for two weeks. It vibrates Pure White Light. We will add several drops of lavender oil to that candle. As you look at this candle flame, you can smell the lavender.

We will now light this candle on the altar in the center of the heart in the name of the I Am That I Am, and in the name of the Paramatman Light. Upon illumination, call upon all those beings and Masters whose pictures and mementos you would like to place on that altar. They come to life and support this creation and the healing that it brings to you.

Now begin breathing by inhaling. Remember to fill your belly first and then push the breath down into your Root Chakra. Then fill your lungs all the way to the top. When it is time to go from inhale to exhale purse out your lips and very slowly let it out. Visualize that you are staring at the beautiful white candle and smelling the lavender oil.

Let us begin to breathe together, Inhale, long and deep, filling every cell of your body. Repeat this mantra in your head as many times as it takes for you to take a long, deep inhalation,

"I Am the Paramatman Light. I breathe the Paramatman Light."

Exhale when you are ready by pursing your lips and slowly letting the air out. Say this mantra as many times as it takes for you to take a long, slow exhalation,

"I become the Paramatman Light. I Am the Paramatman Light."

Do this for four breaths. Then go to your normal breathing. Remember to take three normal breaths. Breath one, inhale and say in your head,

"I Am the Paramatman Light., I breathe the Paramatman Light."

Exhale and say in your head,

"I become the Paramatman Light. I Am the Paramatman Light."

Feel your energy shift as a down-pouring of light begins to shower you. The stillness of the Paramatman Light will bring you peace and harmony.

The white candle is illumined and anchored in the heart bringing energies to purity and innocence.

Phase II: Releasing Dross with the Purple Light of Transmutation: Materializing Spirit

I take you now to the second phase. Let us breathe together one normal breath in front of the altar in the palace of the heart. See that you are moving the white candle to the left hand side, set up a purple candle on the right hand side. This one is like a Pillar of Light which vibrates a purple color. Choose a darker purple. The darker the purple, the more intensity it will have in its transmutation abilities.

We will now light this candle at the altar in the center of the heart, in the name of the I Am That I Am, in the name of the Paramatman Light.

Begin the first deep breath. Do it at your own pace and say,

*"I Am the Paramatman Light. I breathe the Paramatman Light.
I become the Paramatman Light. I Am the Paramatman Light."*

Inhale and exhale deeply. As you move with this breath you may notice that the energy is different. Whereas with the white candle you felt a down-pouring of energies, with this purple candle you may feel a vacuum effect, as though something is being pulled out, now repeat,

*"I Am the Paramatman Light. I breathe the Paramatman Light.
I become the Paramatman Light. I Am the Paramatman Light."*

White flame is pulling energy in; purple flame is letting dross go. One is materializing spirit; the other is spiritizing matter. One is bringing from above to below; the other is releasing from below to above.

Be aware we are in the second phase of the anchoring of the Paramatman Light. When you are ready, go from the full deep breaths into the normal cycle. Something will happen after you anchor the second candle grid. The rhythm becomes smoother, and you may find that your body begins to build itself a rhythm as though it is pulsing as it is releasing. With each pulse, which is connected to the heartbeat, it releases something. With the release, envision that purple colored light is transmuting whatever is being released from your body and aura. Say,

"I Am the Paramatman Light. I breathe the Paramatman Light.
I become the Paramatman Light. I Am the Paramatman Light."

Focus your gaze on the purple candle flame. Say,

"I Am the Paramatman Light. I breathe the Paramatman Light.
I become the Paramatman Light. I Am the Paramatman Light."

Now with the candle grid completely illuminated and anchored in the space of the heart you only need to focus on your physical body. As you repeat this mental exercise, you continue to bring a greater state of purity and innocence to your mind and emotions, releasing the dross, pain and struggles of eons of time. Remember to call upon me to accelerate your healing process.

I bid you great love, I am your own father, Metatron.

CHAPTER V

PROTECTION

We have a beautiful discourse by Mother Mary for the month of May. This is appropriate, as the month of May is Mother Mary's month. The Full Moon of this month is especially powerful because May is also the month of Lord Buddha's celebration. Wesak Festival is an event that is celebrated at the Full Moon in May, honoring Lord Buddha and the energies of compassion and non-violence. Remember Mother Mary and Lord Buddha especially at this time of the year.

During the month of May we can accelerate ourselves on the path to Enlightenment while these two amazing beings over-light our planet with their presence. Calling upon them during meditation and prayer are great tools for higher spiritual growth. If you are awakened any time between 3:30 and 6:30 in the morning, the Masters are calling you to sit in meditation and prayer. Take this opportunity and sit with them in prayer as this is a powerful way to put your needs and desires out to the universe and use the Masters, who are our own older brothers and sisters of Light, to intercede on your behalf. They are offering to take your prayers before the Throne of God. Their intercession can smooth out the path and remove the obstacles. They know what is best for us, and they can help bring greater results than we are able to imagine for ourselves. Specifically, ask Mother Mary and Lord Buddha for their intercession at this time. The healing protection to follow is an excerpt of *Gifts II, Gifts of Practical Guidance for Daily Living: Protection, Healing, Manifestation, Enlightenment* (pages 107-114).

This discourse was given to someone who had received training in healing and recently started her own healing practice. Working on releasing energies from the bodies and emotions of her clients, she had grown weary, fatigued, depressed and experienced a constant low energy state. Her mind was dull and foggy. To function she needed to take naps during the day and go to bed early at night. Mother Mary gave her the Cocoon of Protection healing meditation.

Mother Mary says the purpose of this meditation is to help you open up to receive and to encapsulate your own body and energy in the Pure Light of the I Am, so that you are replenished when you give healing to others. If you do this practice for twenty two days without a break, it becomes part of your own being and it will never leave you. After that, all you need to do is occasionally call upon it to enhance it and to remind yourself that you have protection. It is important to realize that this is given, not just for professional healers, but for all of us. We heal and teach one another through our relationships, during difficult times and good times alike. Sometimes in the sharing of this richness of life, we can become drained. It is at those times we call upon Mother Mary and the Prayer of the Rosary to replenish us.

My Children of Light, I am your Mother Mary.

In the course of this healing, I shall call upon the levels and dimensions of Higher Light to bring you assistance and protection. From now on, whether you are teaching or healing someone in person or from a distance, you will feel yourself refreshed and replenished after the session. This I can do for you when you ask my intercession to bring healing to you and to energize you. The process can be enhanced when you say the Prayer of the Rosary. For this reason I ask you to give great importance to the Prayer of the Rosary and to never be without it. Even if one day you miss the chance to say your prayer, make sure that the next day you pick it up and then say it more intently. The emphasis is not so much on the number of times that you say it but on your continuous connection with me and with the Prayer of the Rosary.

Two purposes are served from working with the Prayer of the Rosary. One is to encapsulate your own energy in the Light of this prayer to raise your vibration to a higher level, and the second is to unite your energies and prayers with the energies of all the Prayers of the Rosary that have ever been said on behalf of humankind. These include those that my Legions and I, Mother Mary, say before the Throne of Grace. The effect is astronomical as many Prayers of the Rosary are constantly performed, and many prayer vigils are constantly held at all times.

When you say the Prayer of the Rosary, I take that prayer and unite it with all the prayers that have ever been said, are now being said and shall ever be said. Then the potency and the intensity of the energy are magnified. The pool of energy of all the Prayers of the Rosary is constantly increased and is available to each of you who say the prayers. Imagine if you say one Prayer of the Rosary, and not just your voice but the voices of multitudes are added to yours.

And with that force, I can accelerate the outcome and bring results to you. With the accumulated power and force of the multitudes through my intercessions, your intention can bear fruit. I am here with you to teach you to protect yourself. To this end, I will invoke Archangel Michael to bring you the Shield of Mercy. The Shield helps raise your own Light energy. As you give this Light to others, you must constantly replenish yourself. The purpose of Archangel Michael's Shield of Mercy is to protect your Light, the Light which you can raise and give to your patients and clients. The Light is raised and maintained within you. Your body can use as much as it needs in any given moment. The Shield will protect the Light from leaking. By encapsulating the Light inside of your own body, you help boost your energy to reach the Higher Realms where you can see, visualize and hear guidance.

The benefits are threefold. First, it is to fill you with Light energy for personal use. This will prevent you from depleting yourself. Second, it is to protect you from draining your energy out of your body or absorbing lower vibrational energies. Finally, it is to enable you to give a higher calibration of the energy to your clients and your patients.

To administer this process, I ask Archangel Michael to place the Shield of Mercy around you. Archangel Michael will call upon his Legions to perform this task. Meanwhile, I send you the energies of the Golden Pink Flame of Divine Love to energize you and to boost your body and beingness. At the same time, I will be calling upon the magnification of the Prayer of the Rosary. This process will take a few minutes.

Meanwhile, I want you to say the Prayer of the Rosary, starting with one Our Father and then ten Hail Marys. Consciously go into the energy of the prayer to receive and absorb the Light. It is beneficial to spend ten minutes each day to repeat this process. Every day set aside some time for meditation and the Prayer of the Rosary. When you learn the prayer by heart you will feel the energies even more. Take a deep breath.

I call upon the presence of Archangel Michael and the Legions of Michael to form a circle of Light around the body of (say your name). I call the presence of all your loved ones and family members to receive from this Shield of Light and Shield of Mercy as well. They will each receive their own Shield of Protection. We call upon the Higher Selves of all to be present. Now call the names of your family members and loved ones that you wish to receive this Shield. For example, *"I call upon my son, James and his Higher Self, to receive the Shield of Mercy."*

The Legions of Michael form circles around each individual's body, with their Swords of Mercy held above their heads. The Sword is drawn out of its sheath, and it emits an Electric Blue Light. The vibration of Electric Blue is much like the sword that Luke Skywalker held in the *Star Wars* movies. The tips of the Swords held by the multitudes of the Legions touch, a dome of Blue Light is created over the head of each individual (say everyone's name). The Blue Light forms a Pillar of Light that surrounds the body of everyone receiving it. The entire circle is filled with pure Electric Blue Light. It is pouring down to everyone's body. Envision that I, Mother Mary, am standing in front of you, facing you and each group member.

My hands are held out. The palms of my hands are upright pointing to the palms of your hands, and my heart is facing your heart. I begin to emit the Golden-Pink Light of Divine Love from the palms of my hands and from my heart chakra.

A dispensation from the Throne of Grace is given to the Masters to bring new energy. It is intended for those working with the Masters. The purpose of this energy ray is to encapsulate you in the higher dimensional energy of Divine Love from the Feminine Principle. The Blue Light emanating from the Sword of Archangel Michael is the Light of Divine Love in its Power Aspect. The Golden-Pink Light from my heart is Divine Love in the Feminine Aspect. Coming from the heart of the Source, these two energies mix, and together they create a balance in your bodies. I will send you the emanation of the feminine Golden Pink Light of Divine Love, and through the Shield of Mercy, Archangel Michael and his Legions send you the Blue Light of Divine Love in its Masculine Form. Energy flows freely from the palm of my hands and from my heart to the palm of your hands and to your heart.

I now call upon Archangel Raphael, and the Legions of Raphael to stand over my presence and to create a Dome of Light with their Swords of Compassion and Divine Love over my head and yours. You will continue to stand under the shower of the Pink Light from me, and the Blue Light from the Legions of Michael. The Blue Light is coming to you from above your head, emanating in the circle where you stand. The Pink Light is coming to you from the palms of my hands and from the center of my heart, as well as from the circle that is created around me by Raphael. Now, we call upon the magnification of the Prayer of the Rosary, recited by the Angelic Forces of Light above my head and yours. We ask for the magnification of all the Light and healing to be received by you and your loved ones.

In the name of the I Am That I Am, I call forth the Shield of Mercy to be lowered from the top of the dome where the tips of the Swords of Mercy are touching and placed around your body. A 24-karat

Liquid Gold Light is poured down. It reaches above your Crown Chakra and begins to form a cocoon around your body, like a Shield of Protection. Your auric field has been gold-leafed. Around the area of your throat, your thymus gland and your chest, the Golden Shield is thicker, two inches, because this is the area where you deplete yourself. This is the area where lower vibrations can penetrate. When we form the thick shield around your chest, any energies of lower vibration will be transmuted upon contact and turned into Pure White Light. In the areas where you simply need an encapsulation of your own energy, this Shield is thinner; in areas where you need extra protection, the Shield is thicker. As this Gold is poured over the surface of your skin, it cocoons your body and your energy body around your aura.

Breathe deeply now. The Golden Pink that your Mother Mary and Archangel Raphael are sending you is mixing with the Pure Electric Blue Light that Archangel Michael is bringing to you from the heart core of God, the Undifferentiated Source. The Divine Principle of Feminine and the Divine Principle of Masculine mix and merge. The Blue and Pink, with the Gold to seal it, unite in your energy field. The Golden Cocoon of Light, the Golden Shield, will protect each one of you from this moment on from any lower vibration and from depletion.

Take a deep breath and become aware of your body and your energy. I thank Archangel Michael and his Legions and Archangel Raphael and her Legions. And in this instance, I call the Masculine Aspect of Lord Michael and Feminine Aspect of Archangel Raphael. Raphael is the Angel of Ministration, Angel of Healing, Angel of Music, Angel of Freedom. Michael is the Angel of Mercy, Angel of Protection, Angel of Prevention from all harm. We thank them for their presence.

I hold you in my own arms. I am your Mother Mary.

PRAYER OF THE ROSARY

Three versions of the Prayer of the Rosary are included here, the traditional Christian, the original Essene version and the New Age version. Recite whichever one that resonates with you. You are encouraged to follow Mother Mary's request to, *"Pray. Pray. Pray."*

To recite one round of the Prayer of the Rosary, you need to say one Our Father followed by ten Hail Marys, and then repeat this sequence five times. This is the simplified version which is a good start. Before you start, sit in meditation, still your mind and say, *"I offer this prayer for peace on Earth and for my personal intentions (state your intentions). I unite myself in prayer with Mother Mary and ask for her help and the intercession of all the Masters of Light to magnify these prayers in the name of the I Am That I Am."* Then begin by one Our Father, ten Hail Marys and one Glory Be. Do this five times, and you will have completed one round of the Prayer of the Rosary.

Our Father (Traditional Christian)
Our Father who art in Heaven, hallowed be Thy name. Thy Kingdom come, Thy will be done on Earth as it is in Heaven. Give us this day our daily bread and forgive us our trespasses, as we forgive those who trespass against us. Lead us not into temptation and deliver us from evil. For Thine is the kingdom and the power and glory, now and forever.
Amen.

Hail Mary (Traditional Christian)
Hail Mary, full of grace, the Lord is with Thee. Blessed are Thou among women and blessed is the fruit of Thy womb, Jesus. Holy Mary, mother of God, pray for us sinners now and at the hour of our death.
Amen.

Glory Be (Traditional Christian)

Glory be to the Father and the Son and the Holy Spirit. As it was in the beginning, is now and ever shall be.

Amen.

If you feel drawn, you may do as many repetitions as you can. To obtain a rosary and the long version of the prayers, you can stop at a religious store or a Catholic church. Many people use their fingers to count the numbers as they say the prayer, and it works just as well.

Below is the Essene version of the prayer of Our Father and Our Mother as stated in the teachings of Master Jesus and translated by Edmond Bordeaux Szekely in *The Essene Gospel of Peace.* The Our Father portion of the prayer is very similar to the traditional Christian prayer. However, as you see, the Our Mother portion is completely missing from the traditional Christian prayer. It is an important and integral piece for these reasons:

1. It restores the balance of Feminine and Masculine by acknowledging the Mother Aspect and holding her in respect and reverence alongside of the Father Aspect.

2. It restores balance to Mother Earth and invokes the Angels of Earthly Mother to bless us and Earth together.

3. It reconnects us, the human beings, with our Mother Earth and brings healing to Earth and to us. It can serve as a reminder that as our Mother, we must hold her in respect and reverence and treat her as we ideally would treat our human mothers.

4. It will enable us to enter into the flow of abundance and assistance which comes to us from Earth. After all, let

us be reminded that all the resources which bring us comfort, luxury, peace and harmony are from Earth.

Our Father (Essene)

Our Father which art in Heaven, hallowed be Thy name. Thy kingdom come. Thy will be done on Earth as it is in Heaven. Give us this day our daily bread. And forgive us our debts, as we forgive our debtors. And lead us not into temptation, but deliver us from evil. For Thine is the kingdom, the power and the glory, forever.

Amen.

Our Mother (Essene)

Our Mother which art upon Earth, hallowed be Thy name. Thy kingdom come, and Thy will be done in us, as it is in Thee. As Thou send every day Thy angels, send them to us also. Forgive us our sins, as we atone all our sins against Thee. And lead us not into sickness, but deliver us from all evil. For Thine is the Earth, the body and the health.

Amen.

Rosary of the New Age

Hail Mother, full of grace, the Lord is with Thee. Blessed art Thou amongst women and blessed is the fruit of Thy womb I Am. Hold for us now the immaculate concept of our true God Reality from this moment unto our eternal Ascension in the Light of the I Am That I Am.

CHAPTER VI

HEALING, COMPASSION AND MERCY

In this Grid of Light Quan Yin calls to three of the Angelic Forces, known as the Angels of the Thrones, and Guardian Angels of the Four Directions. Uriel, Raphael, Michael together with Gabriel stand in the four directions and guard the four corners of Earth. Uriel stands in the North, Raphael in the East, Michael in the South and Gabriel in the West. These four also guard the Throne of God also known as the *"Throne of Grace."* They stand in four directions around the Throne. They are known to be Angelic Forces of great power and Light as they are able to withstand the intensity of the Light at the Throne of Grace.

In this meditational exercise, Quan Yin is calling upon three Angels of the Throne, together with two Personal Guardian Angels. The Guardian Angel of Intellect is the protector of the mental body and, therefore, our mental processes are guided and guarded by this angel. The other is the Guardian Angel of Emotions. This Angel is the Guardian of the Emotional body and in charge of harnessing the unruly and unguarded emotions which can get us into trouble and lead us into hasty decisions. Quan Yin and these five angels, make a Grid of Light.

Archangel Michael is the protector of all humankind. He can cut the cords of karma and karmic entanglement from our lives upon asking. This act alone can accelerate us to greater success both in the mundane world and in our spiritual endeavors. No good comes from keeping karmic relationships in our lives, whether they are with people, places or things. If a thing is good for us, it will stay in our life after the cords are cut. If a place is conducive to our growth and our evolution, we will stay in that place, be it a room, a house, a job, a town, a city or a country. If not, we are better off leaving the room, the house, the job, the town or the country.

If a relationship is enhancing, then it is worth keeping. If not, better to be done with the relationship and move on to bigger and better things. As human beings, we have a Divine Purpose to serve. Relationships can either promote and enhance our Divine Purpose or delay it. If they are delaying us, then we are only prolonging the agony of remaining in this cycle of birth, death and rebirth until we learn the lessons. Rest assured that if a relationship is pleasant and heart warming, loving and nurturing, they would not be in the category of karmic ones. Karmic entanglements, as the name implies, are those which hold us in their grip at the cost of our time, energy, money and sometimes sanity.

Last but not least, Quan Yin embraces us in her own web of compassion and mercy to protect us and bring us the Light of these two qualities. We do need compassion to cope with all events and issues and mercy to enhance our lives. As a child, I remember hearing, *"When you stand before God, do not ask for judgment, ask for mercy."* We not only ask to be merciful to others but we also ask for mercy to shower upon us from heavens above and make our lives sweet and enjoyable. I wish you a most enjoyable experience in performing this exercise.

My Children of Light, I am Quan Yin.

I will give you a Grid of Light to bring strength and courage in these days as we enter summer, starting on Summer Solstice (June 19-21). This Grid will help you to choose progress, to move forward and to serve the Light. Sit with me and bring your mind to stillness. Take a deep, long breath as I begin to invoke the following Angelic Forces of Light:

I call forth the presence of Archangel Michael, Archangel Uriel, Archangel Raphael, Mother Mary and Quan Yin to create a Grid of Light around you. Envision Archangel Uriel standing directly in front of you sending a Golden Yellow Ray of Inner Light to your heart and your body. I ask Archangel Uriel to help release all karmic entanglements and to help you serve your Divine Purpose. Take a deep breath and pause for a moment. At this point, I call upon your soul essence to come forth.

I ask that the soul essence now merge with the personality and receive the Flame of Inner Light from Archangel Uriel. Pause and take a deep breath.

Visualize that the Flame is placed by Archangel Uriel in your Heart Chakra. See it to be fully ignited, illuminating your Heart Chakra. Once the personality and soul merge, there will be a feeling of homecoming. Then the personality no longer feels lonely or left out because the personality will begin to fully realize the purpose for being here on Earth and know your presence on Earth is important and your Light is great. Realizing the nature of its Divine Purpose, the personality becomes joyful that it has found its purpose, and allows it to be aligned with the Divine Purpose. The personality would then want nothing more but to serve the Divine Purpose. That is a noble place to be in, a noble Truth to experience. People come to Earth for many rounds of incarnation, taking physical embodiments without realizing that they have a Divine Purpose to fulfill. There is a Soul Purpose or Soul Mission to be served. This Soul Purpose is of the utmost importance and supersedes that of the personality and that of the consciousness of the body and mind. Take a deep breath.

I now ask Archangel Michael to cut all the cords of karmic entanglement from you, all those cords which you may have, knowingly or unknowingly, created with people, places and things. As Archangel Michael cuts the cords, I ask that he illumines the pathway for your soul growth and your worldly success and removes all obstacles from your path. Walking on this path, you would fully and completely embody your Divine Purpose and be supported by the Light that is shinning upon you from the Higher Realms. You will also have the pathways cleared for success in all your worldly endeavors. Take a deep breath.

I now call forth your two Guardian Angels, the Guardian Angel who deals with the intellect and the Guardian Angel who deals with emotions, to come forward. I ask the Guardian Angel of Emotions to hold your left hand and the Guardian Angel of Intellect to hold your right hand. I ask these Guardian Angels to give you mental and emotional support, strength, courage, power, stamina and zest for life.

I ask these two Guardian Angels to walk on this path alongside of you, to watch over you and to heal your emotional and mental bodies. They will guide you to cope with all emotional and intellectual matters. I ask that they show you the path which you must walk upon. The healing restores wholeness and perfection for you. I ask the two guardians to continue to walk alongside of you from this point on and to guide you at all times. I ask these two Guardian Angels to teach you their wisdom in dreamtime while you sleep.

I ask that Archangel Raphael, Angel of Healing, to assist these two angels in restoring you to full perfected health and wholeness. You can then become a role model for all those who follow you. I ask that with the help of your guardian angels, your Light may illuminate others and expand the consciousness of all. On behalf of those who are receptive to this Light, we ask that they be connected to their own mental/emotional Guardian Angels. I ask Archangel Raphael to continue to pour the Golden-Pink Light of Loving Compassion upon you to transmute the pollution from all your energy bodies and to restore health and wholeness. Take a deep breath.

Visualize Archangel Raphael standing in the formation of the Grid of Light beaming you the Golden-Pink Light. Uriel is much larger in stature and in power than your two Guardian Angels. The Guardian

Angels will continue to walk by your side and restore you to the original state of perfected health and wholeness, as intended for you by the Divine Plan. I ask all of this in the name of the I Am That I Am for your benefit and the benefit of all the souls whom you may touch. I ask the Light of the I Am That I Am to clear all the obstacles from your path and from the path of everyone you touch.

I ask this in the name of the I Am That I Am, from all The Thrones of Higher Power, The Throne of The Undifferentiated Source, the Throne of Absolute and the Abode of the Divine Mother.

Now I offer you my own web of compassion and mercy. Imagine yourself being showered with deep Blue and Pink-Purple Light. Deep blue is the energy of Divine Mercy and the Pink-Purple is the Light of compassion. Receive and bathe in these energies and visualize them forming a web of Light around you and around the formation of Light.

Sit with me in these energies for a moment. Allow me to fill your heart with joy and gratitude. Let me remind you that you are not alone. You are loved and cherished. Feel the strength from these Archangelic Forces and the healing that is administered to you. Intend for all souls to benefit from this energy and welcome them to receive it. This experience is registered into your cell structure as part of your own personal grid; to heal you, restore you to wholeness, and to illumine the pathway ahead of you for your Divine Purpose to unfold. Take a deep breath and pause for a moment.

We ask the Masters of Light to help and assist in making this Light available to all souls, especially the young people. Those who do not have goals or disciplined focus on achieving goals; those unaware of the Path of Light and all opportunities available to them, are now called to find this Grid of Light. They can now tap into this Grid of Light and awaken to the presence, the benefit and the protection from their own Guardian Angels, Archangel Uriel, Archangel Raphael, and Archangel Michael. They may now receive the Inner Light, Divine Mercy, and healing which they need to restore them to perfect health and wholeness. I ask you to pray for all souls to find their path through the Light and healing from these angels.

Quan Yin's Grid of Healing, Compassion and Mercy with Guardian Angels of Intellect & Emotions and Archangels Uriel, Raphael and Michael

You will gain merits by such an intention and will help the world. Every time a new member of the Community of Light finds their own path in this way, you will gain merits and the path becomes further illumined for the multitudes and masses. We invite all souls to join us in this healing. We set out intentions that every soul who connects energetically to this Grid of Light be guided by the Masters and the Guardian Angels of Light.

I hold you in my own heart with great love. Call upon me when you need me, I will be there for you.

I am your mother, Quan Yin. So it is.

CHAPTER VII

FINANCIAL ABUNDANCE AND RELATIONSHIPS

A candle grid is an important and potent way to get results and give momentum to our lives, especially when there is stagnation. It can create energy flow and remove obstacles. This is a candle grid which Quan Yin has given for two important areas of our lives, money and relationships. What is special about this one is that she addresses both of these issues in one candle grid.

Practically everyone has to face these two issues at some point in their lives. It is bad enough when there is a lack in one of these areas. It becomes even more difficult when there is lack in both areas. By focusing on both issues in one exercise, Quan Yin is giving us a lot to work with. Coupling two great invocations in conjunction with the candle grid, she helps make it more potent and effective. For those of you who are already in a romantic relationship, use it to bring greater love and Light into the existing partnership. It can also be used for work related, family related, parent-child, sibling, extended family, friends, and spiritual and social group member relationships.

Candles are important manifestation tools. Manifestation in the material realm always depends on the partnership of the human mind and will, with the four basic elements, Earth, Air, Water, and Fire. Candles hold the energy of all the four elements. The flame represents the Fire element. The beeswax or paraffin wax represents the Earth element, and it also contains the Water. Therefore, the Water element too is in the candle. The candle can only be lit in the presence of Air; the smoke coming from the burning flame is also representative of the Air element.

The combined energies, of focus from our mind and will-power from our will center or Solar Plexus, in conjunction with the four elements, give us the momentum we need to move stagnant energies out, remove obstacles from our path and materialize our intentions. Remember, energy follows intent.

My Beloved Children of Light, I am Quan Yin.

I offer you a grid that will bring you a loving relationship as well as spiritual power and abundance. You can keep this grid going for anywhere from three weeks to three months or more. It will be beneficial and effective to continue to light your candles daily for three months. Therefore, plan to set your grid up with larger candles if you choose to do this. Start with three deep Nile blue pillar candles (3" x 9"). These three candles represent power to bring you financial abundance. It is the color which radiates Divine Power and enables you to build up your own personal as well as spiritual power. You can use that power to attract nurturing relationships and financial abundance.

To remove obstacles from your path, to enhance existing relationships or to start new ones, use three white pillar candles (3" x 9"). Take a piece of white poster board and cut it to the size of a 15" square. With a gold-tipped pen, draw two equilateral triangles on the poster board. The length of each side is nine inches. The two triangles merge into each other to form a six pointed star. Use the gold-tipped pen to draw the star. Once this is drawn, place the three blue candles at the three points of the triangle which is pointing upwards. Place the three white candles at the three points of the triangle which is pointing downwards. Once they are all placed on the board, the candles should be alternating blue and white and positioned at the points of the golden star. In the middle of this grid, at the very center of the star, draw a sign of infinity, approximately three inches from point to point, with the gold pen. Fill the entire symbol of infinity with cinnamon. Cinnamon attracts the objects of your desires to you and transmutes negativity and obstacles. It helps to bring completion to the task at hand and provide final closure.

Charging your Candle Grid

To imbue the candle grid with energy and intention, take the first blue candle, at the top point of the grid, hold it up and say, *"In the name of the I Am That I Am, I invoke the love and the Light and the coming forth of a soul mate, my companion, my loving partner. I ask this in the name of the I Am That I Am."* For those who are already in a relationship you can say: *"In the name of the I Am That I Am, I invoke love and Light in my present relationship with (name)."*

Place this candle back at the point of the triangle, and moving clockwise, pick up the next one, a white candle, and say, *"In the name of the I Am That I Am, I call forth the removal of all obstacles and all delays and for purity and innocence to be restored to me. Through the return of purity and innocence, I ask for abundance, prosperity, financial comfort and luxury. In the name of the I Am That I Am, it is given. So it is. Amen."* Place the candle back on the point of your golden grid on top of the white poster board.

Go around the grid clockwise, repeat the same process for each of the remaining blue and white candles and say the invocation for each one. The prayer of purity and innocence and the return to financial abundance with the white, and the prayer of companionship and love and the coming together with the soul mate (friend, family member, etc.) for the blue candles.

Once all candles are placed back on the Grid, take a pinch of cinnamon and join the points of each candle to make a circle. You draw this circle by hand with cinnamon. With this act, you are encompassing the energy of this entire grid with cinnamon to absorb all of your intentions and prayers that you have put into the grid. The cinnamon will clear the obstacles from the grid and from your life and will cleanse and hold the intention for infinite love, wisdom, and financial abundance to come to you from the universe. Take a deep breath.

Sit quietly and say your intentions; for partnership, friendship, or any other type relationship in this life, resolution of finances, comfort and luxury for myself, my companion, my family and my loved ones and say the invocations, in the name of the I Am That I Am.

Repeat your intentions. At night the energy invoked by the mantra in the room will flood the energy of the body during sleep.

Continue to repeat this process over the next three months or longer. Replace old candles with new ones as each set ends. Keep a small amount of wax from each old candle and put it inside of each new corresponding candle. This will ensure the continuation of the energy to filter through into the new candles in the grid. By focusing intently on this grid, you will bring new Life Force and Light, greater joy, love, financial abundance and resolution into your life and existence. Begin and end each invocation with I Am That I Am. Call upon Quan Yin to be the guardian of your candle grid. Call upon your favorite Masters, guides and guardian angels to watch over you and bring your intentions to bear fruit.

I am your mother, Quan Yin. So it is.

Summary

Materials Needed

- white poster board cut to a 15" square
- 3 deep blue (Nile blue) pillar candles (3" x 9"to represent power to bring a loving companion and financial abundance
- 3 white pillar candles (3" x 9") for removal of obstacles and return to purity and innocence
- gold-ink marker, gel or felt pen
- ruler and protractor or 11" plate (to draw circle)
- cinnamon attracts the objects of your desires and transmutes negativity

Instructions for Creating the Candle Grid

1. On a piece of white poster board, with gold ink, draw two nine-inch equilateral triangles, intertwined to make a Star of David.

2. Draw a large sign of infinity at the center of the star (no smaller than three inches edge to edge) and fill the loops with cinnamon.

3. Place three deep Nile blue candles (3" x 9") at the points of the triangle which point upward (to represent Divine Power).

4. Place three white candles (3" x 9") at the points of the downward triangle (to represent return to purity and innocence).

Energizing the Candle Grid

Pick up the first blue candle from the grid. Hold it up and say your mantra three times. Moving clockwise, pick up the first white candle, hold it up and say your mantra three times.

Repeat this for all the candles.

Lighting the Candle Grid

Light the candles, starting at the top and moving clockwise. Sit and meditate while you focus on your intentions for this grid, such as abundance, spiritual purity and innocence, a loving and nurturing relationship, etc.

Light your candles every day for three months to give you momentum. It will help speed up the movement of old energy out of your life and bring the Light of new energy into your life.

When the first round of candles melt down, discard the leftovers, but save some wax from the old Grid to add to the new one for continuation of the energy. Clean your poster board and repeat from step four onwards. If your board is smeared with candle wax, you can start a new grid and put the old grid's cinnamon back on the newly drawn poster board. When you are completely finished with your grid, you can throw the cinnamon in your flower or vegetable garden, offering it to Earth, or you can take it to a body of flowing water and offer it to the water (ocean, stream, whatever is nearby or convenient, but not a stagnant body of water like a pond). The idea is that your intention will continue to flow with the water which is moving. The leftover candle wax can be discarded with your poster board. Alternatively, you can burn your poster board to bring the desires to yourself more quickly. As you burn it, say, *"I burn this grid and I ask the four elements to bring me the objects of my desires faster, in the name of the I Am That I Am."* You may also burn it in thanksgiving for the objects of your desires being manifest in your life.

CHAPTER VIII

1st, 2nd and 3rd Levels of Initiation

Christ Maitreya is the World Teacher. He is the leader of a hierarchy of Masters known as the Masters of Wisdom. The office of the World Teacher is a highly elevated office in the hierarchies of the Ascended Masters and is responsible for bringing Earth into the New Age. Christ Maitreya is in charge of the ascension of Earth and the elevation of all souls to reach Enlightenment. Many of the ascended Masters work directly with Christ Maitreya. Archangel Michael, Master Jesus, Quan Yin, Mother Mary as well as Sanat Kumara are but a few. The living Masters and Avatars are also believed to be in contact with Christ Maitreya.

It is a great blessing and good fortune that Christ Maitreya has taken physical embodiment on Earth at this present time. It is an extraordinary event when a Master from such a highly illumined rank decides to dive back into the density of this third dimensional reality. The great sacrifice that Christ Maitreya makes to lower his vibration in order to take physical embodiment merits the respect of all great beings of Light. I have witnessed many of the Masters, especially Sanat Kumara and Metatron, defer to him and his decisions without exception. Because of his sacrifice and his presence at this dimensional level, he is by far the most effective, powerful and high ranking official from the hierarchy available to us, not only energetically but physically. There is evidence that he has taken residence in the Middle Eastern section of London's Marble Arch. He has made a few appearances in large and small crowds. One of these was in the year 1988 in Kenya to a crowd of many thousands. At this event, a famous picture was taken of him walking through the masses in white robes and head dress.

I have had my own personal experiences with the World Teacher. Some of these I have recounted in a chapter devoted to Christ Maitreya in my book, *Gifts III, Journeys into the Inner Realms of Consciousness*, by Nasrin Safai. I have included an excerpt from that chapter here.

"Christ Maitreya is our World Teacher and the leader of the Masters of Wisdom and their disciples. He is the planetary Christ in that he carries the consciousness of the Christed Self, or the True Self — the Enlightened Self. His presence on Earth at this juncture of Earth's evolution is to assist the Masters of Light to bring their disciples, those who have already awakened to their divinity, to Mastery and to awaken the spiritually un-awakened souls to the consciousness of the Divine Spark." pp. 27, ibid.

His desire is that we say the prayer of the Great Invocation as many times as we can day and night and for all of us to share the energy of his presence with others through this prayer. The Great Invocation was given by a Tibetan Master called Djwal Khul to Alice Bailey, a famous channel in 1945. Christ Maitreya imbues it with his own energy to increase its potency by reciting the Great Invocation daily in the sacred language of Light. We can connect to Christ Maitreya through the recitation of this invocation. See page xii of this book. Christ Maitreya also asks that you do the meditation included below.

A great book on Christ Maitreya and the Masters of Wisdom, with pictures of Christ Maitreya's appearance in Kenya in 1988, is *Extraordinary Times, Extraordinary Being: Experiences of an American Diplomat with Maitreya and the Masters of Wisdom* by Wayne S. Peterson. www.waynepeterson.com. The image of Christ Maitreya is courtesy of Share International.

Beloveds of my own heart, I am Metatron. Take a deep breath with me.

Focus your attention on your cosmic heart. I will take you before the presence of Christ Maitreya to receive an initiation. When you awaken to your Divine Light, you begin to walk on the path of spiritual evolution to reach Enlightenment. The Master who is the guiding Light to walk you along that path is Christ Maitreya. It is the responsibility of the World teacher to guide and train every awakened soul and to administer the First, Second and Third levels of Initiation. At the point of the 3rd Initiation, the initiate will receive guidance both from Christ Maitreya and Sanat Kumara, the Planetary Logos. Levels of initiation are the steps which every initiate must take to reach Mastery and Enlightenment.

Mastery is reached at the point of the 5th Initiation. From that point on an initiate is walking on the path of full Enlightenment. Each of the events above is a Landmark. Every individual has their own unique way of reaching and moving through these Landmarks. Yet everyone who steps on this path must go through the process in the same way. I will take you all through a meditational journey; we will go before the presence of the World Teacher and you will receive First, Second or Third Initiation. The level of your initiation depends on your state of wakefulness and the Quotient of Light which you are capable of holding.

Going through the levels of initiation does not automatically entitle you to complete that step or phase of spiritual attainment. You must prove your ability to reach and maintain the Quotient of Light necessary to function at these levels of initiation.

Grace is a wonderful quality which is received through bestowal. Grace takes you beyond merits. Merits are earned. You must work to earn merits to move to a higher state and to climb the spiritual ladder. However, the ladder can be climbed much faster through the bestowal of Grace. Remember that intention is everything. You can intend to receive the Grace to accelerate you in reaching these levels and to help you maintain your Quotient of Light.

At this present juncture, the state of Earth has merited a dispensation for the bestowal of Grace for those who ask for acceleration on the path to Enlightenment. We have come to the end point for this age, known as Kali Yuga, the age of chaos and darkness. We are standing at the gateway of entry into the Seventh Golden Age. To enter, we must increase the Quotient of Light for Earth and all souls. This requires increasing the available number of initiates at all levels from 1st, 2nd, 3rd, and 4th to Mastery; an event which is the prime focus of the Masters of Wisdom and Christ Maitreya. When you choose to accelerate yourself on the path, you too will participate in this great feat. You become the beacons of Light and spearheads for the enfoldment of the Seventh Golden Age. The physical presence of Christ Maitreya on Earth is to facilitate this feat.

Christ Maitreya will initiate you to the level most appropriate for you. If you have indeed reached the point where you are able to receive the higher initiations, you will be able to see Christ Maitreya invite you to go before Sanat Kumara, the Planetary Logos.

Sanat Kumara is the Guardian of the Fourth and Fifth Initiations. Christ Maitreya and Sanat Kumara work with you from the point of your 3rd Initiation on. You can ask for Grace from both these great beings to accelerate you on your path to Enlightenment. I, Metatron, will intercede on your behalf before both of them. You can ask them in my name when requesting their Grace. Say: *"In the name of Metatron, I call forth the presence of Christ Maitreya, the World Teacher and Sanat Kumara, the Planetary Logos, to bestow upon me the Grace of acceleration and the steps of Initiation to higher Light from this day on. So it is."*

Say this invocation at all times and sincerely mean it from the core of your heart. Let your sincerity and your love, melt their hearts. Appeal to their compassion; believe it can be done. As the old adage goes; "where there is a will, there is a way." I will show you the way; you will it to come true for you. Take a deep breath.

MEDITATIONAL JOURNEY

Visualize yourself standing inside the Pillar of Pure Light. All around you Light is emanating. The Pillar extends to the Heavenly Realms of Light. We will travel inside the Pillar of Light to reach the etheric Temple of Hope. This is the etheric retreat of Christ Maitreya. Its location is over Cape of Hope in the area of New Zealand. However, this is not an earthly plane but an etheric one. You can only go there, if invited. You must be brought encased in the Light of a great being. I encase you in my own Light and bring you to this magical place. After the first introduction through a Master, you may come again by calling upon the Master who brought you the first time and by visualizing yourself encased inside of Him. You must however build up your Light to enter inside the Temple.

To facilitate this, I ask you to visualize yourself wrapped inside the Mantle of Metatron. This Mantle is made of shimmering Blue Light interspersed with Platinum stardust. See yourself immersed inside the Mantle as we go through the gateways of the Temple. Once inside you will find yourself in a Great Hall. The Light emanating from every direction is a Teal Blue-Green color. This is the signature color of Christ Maitreya. Allow your body to absorb this Light and become accustomed to the beat of the energy. There is a pulsing sensation to this energy.

You may experience pressure in your temples and in the area of your cosmic and personal heart chakras. This sensation is a sign that energy is moving through you to increase your Quotient of Light.

Look to the center of this great hall where a round raised stage, like a small dance floor, is erected. Walk to that stage. You will notice that the Teal-Blue Light becomes thicker in the center. As you get closer, you will notice that Christ Maitreya is standing at the center of this stage. You will begin to notice his features as you get closer. A force moves you to bow down and kneel at his feet. His right hand is laid over your forehead and crown chakra as you bow down before him. An electric charge of Light moves from his hand to your head; a wave of energy moves down your head to your shoulders, to your chest, energizing all the chakras of your body. Your heart is pounding and your ears are hot. Become still and begin to breathe deeply.

He will beckon you to rise and stand in front of him. Then, he may choose to place the palm of his hand in various chakras of your body, transferring his Light to you. He may lay his hand over your channeling chakra to enhance your ability to receive verbal communication from the inner realms.

He may choose to tell you what level of initiation you are receiving. He may talk to you about your future, about your life, your work or whatever he may choose. If you have difficulty hearing him, then say: *"I ask, through your Grace and intercession, for all that you choose to give me. You are my Teacher and the Savior of my world. I offer myself in service to you. I ask you to open my energy centers to your Light. Remove all obstacles from my path of Mastery and Enlightenment. I offer myself in trust and surrender to you."* Stay for a moment to allow him to administer to you all that he chooses to bestow upon you. Take a deep breath.

You may notice that Sanat Kumara is approaching the stage at this point. Sanat Kumara will come forward and stand by Christ Maitreya's side. Bow down and lower your head in obeisance to him. He may place his hand over your head in the same way that Christ Maitreya did. Pause and receive the energies from him. If you are unable to see or feel Sanat Kumara's presence, then say: *"I ask the intercession of Christ Maitreya and Sanat Kumara in my life. I ask, through their grace, for the bestowal of the highest level of initiation that my body and my being can withstand. I ask that I maintain what I receive and rise up in power and might to serve the Light. If I am at this present moment unable to receive the highest initiation, I request that I may be accelerated on my path of spiritual evolution to Mastery and Enlightenment through the Grace of Christ Maitreya and Sanat Kumara with intercession from Metatron."* Pause and be still to receive the blessing and Grace. Take a deep breath.

Now it is time to take our leave. Bow down in gratitude and offer thanks for this great opportunity. We now leave the stage and move out of this Great Hall and out of the gateway of the Temple. We spiral down to reach back to this third dimensional reality and the consciousness of our bodies.

You may repeat this exercise daily for twenty two days until you master it. After that, you may repeat it occasionally to accelerate yourself further on the path of Enlightenment and in your service to the Light.

Remember that you can always call upon me, Metatron, in all your endeavors. I am always at your service. With great love, I hold you in my own heart.

I am your very own Metatron.

CHAPTER IX

RETURN OF THE LORDS OF LIGHT

In September, we celebrate Fall Equinox. Master Jesus is offering a meditational Grid of Light. He has specially requested that we say the invocations and perform this meditation from September to December and into the New Year. These are important months for growth and acceleration from a personal and a planetary point of view. The Light Quotient for this planet and for all humankind is increasing. Many Portals of Light are opening up from higher planetary bodies like our sun and other suns of this galaxy. All this Light is coming to Earth to help us move to a new phase of our evolution where peace and harmony will replace the chaos and confusion. Reaching a permanent state of peace and harmony is our right as human beings. It is the Divine Plan that we live in that state at all times.

In the course of many civilizations throughout the history of Earth, there have been such times. The Seven Lords of Light and their leader, the Maha Lord of Light, are the guardians of Light for this planet. When the Quotient of Light is maintained at a certain level, the result is peace and harmony. When it falls, chaos and confusion abound. The presence of the Lords of Light in positions of leadership and guardianship over Earth make certain a constant state of peace and harmony. This is why Master Jesus asks that we constantly repeat the intention for the return of guardianship of the Lords of Light. The great news is that the Lords of Light have already returned to take their positions as guardians!

A few of us have been diligently involved in performing this and other similar exercises, practically around the clock, and the positive changes are obvious to us. The Lords of Light shine their Light upon our planet as we speak. Your participation in these invocations and the practice of these exercises will raise the Light inside our beingness and upon the planet. This happens because we will it so. It will enhance the Quotient of Light and accelerate the involvement of these great beings in our planet. More on the Lords of Light can be found in *Path to Enlightenment Book II* and *Book III.*

Many Masters of Light under the leadership of Christ Maitreya are planning to physically walk on Earth at this critical time. It is therefore of utmost importance for us to participate in this great endeavor. We can add our efforts to that of the Masters by saying the prayer of The Great Invocation and performing all individual and group ceremonies, rituals, pujas, invocations, meditations, and any other exercise which facilitate greater Light to shine upon the planet and make the job easier for the Masters responsible for this enormous task. Master Jesus has given us one example. He is requesting that we perform this meditational exercise at least once daily and as many more times each day as we choose to.

Together we can form a powerful group reaching all across the globe to invoke and attract greater Light to shine upon Mother Earth, and our own bodies. In this way we can benefit all souls and shift the consciousness of all souls in the direction of spiritual growth and Enlightenment. By spiritual law, we always receive ten fold in return for what we extend to others. I pray that you reap the harvest a hundred fold and thousand fold in return for the Light that you shine upon us all.

Master Jeshua also offers the following intention that may be added to all your prayers as well, *"When the Masters of Light walk upon this planet, I ask for the grace to walk amongst them, to serve them, and to be their disciple. I further ask for the merit to recognize their true identity when I am placed amongst them."*

This reminds me of a story. A few years ago I participated in a four day conference given by an internationally known spiritual leader who was a devoted disciple of Sai Baba, a living Master or avatar. The conference was attended by many hundreds of people. It was evident that there were many opposing energies present during the course of the workshop which made the task of the leadership difficult. On the last day of the conference, I happened to arrive after the session had started. I rushed in to show my security badge at the entrance of the conference hall. Once there, I noticed a young man seated on the floor, on a purple cloth with rose petals strewn all around him. He had a face that was shining with Light. His hair was in dread locks with a bandana wrapped around his head and his attire was that of a young hippie. I felt love for this young man, yet the thought on my mind was, *"How did he pass through security in this attire and be allowed to sit on the floor right in front of the conference room?"* I gave no further thought to the matter and went inside. At the final conclusion of the conference the facilitator asked how many people had seen the young man seated outside. A few people raised their hands. He then proceeded to tell everyone that this young man had appeared from nowhere and disappeared to nowhere. No member of the security had seen him pass through and after he disappeared, a trail of rose petals and sweet scent of roses was left behind.

The facilitator then told everyone that he had received inner guidance about this man, that he was a messenger from the Masters and Sai Baba. His presence was to confirm that in spite of all the difficulties caused by the opposing factions, the Masters were pleased with the work of all the attendees. His presence was to bless everyone and confirm the success of the conference. It was only then that I recalled my own personal experience of the incident. At that moment all I could think about was how I missed the chance of a lifetime. If I had the presence of mind, I would have taken time to be with this sweet soul and receive a direct blessing. My prayer is that when you are blessed to be in physical presence of a Master, you will recognize his or her true identity. I have included the prayer of The Great Invocation which is a prayer to invoke the return of Christ Maitreya, in the Introduction. Christ Maitreya is the World Teacher and is known to have been the guiding force behind Master Jesus' teachings.

The following is a meditational exercise in which you are empowering yourself to carry and collect greater Light into your body through your Solar Plexus. Even though Jesus gives the entire exercise in a paragraph, I remind you to be patient and gentle with yourself. It may take a while before you can see the Ball of Light fully formed around your body. If you can only take it to a certain size the first try, that is perfectly fine. Jeshua gives us a shortcut by offering to do it on our behalf. That is certainly a great help and will accelerate you. Your own effort will bear fruit over time and the satisfaction is great. I say this from my experience with different people. Everyone has their own pace. I love it when someone says, *"Today I was only able to get my Ball to grow to the size of an orange. I will try harder and I will get it to grow more next time."* This is more meaningful and consistent than when someone puts the last ounce of their effort into making the orange ball large once and gets so weary of the whole process that they give up. Although all efforts are commendable, I would ask you to be gentle and loving to yourself. The reward of knowing that you make a great difference is wonderful. I wish you great success in fully accomplishing Master Jeshua's request through this exercise in the days ahead.

Adonai My Beloveds. I am Jeshua Ben Joseph.

I ask you all at the time of Fall Equinox (September 19-22) to perform this meditational invocation and to continue through the end of the year. As you practice this exercise, the energies will intensify and the benefits will magnify for you and the planet as well as all souls. You are the Light that shines upon this planet. With your Light, the Masters will relinquish the darkness. The Seven Lords of Light, who are the true Guardians of Light, will then return to become the true Guardians of Earth; as was originally intended by Divine Providence for this planet and all souls. Remember to repeat these three intentions at all times,

- *"Annihilation of evil and all acts of evil;*
- *Release of all darkness from the bodies of Earth and all souls;*
- *Return of the Lords of Light to take guardianship of the planet and all souls."*

Say these three intentions at all times throughout the course of the next four months. The time-frame between the Fall Equinox (Sept. 19-22) and the Winter Solstice (Dec. 19-22) is a crucial time. Many Portals of Light are open during this three month phase. Focus on calling the Masters of Light and invoking the Lords of Light to come forth as the Guardians of Light to Earth. This will trigger greater Light to shine upon the planet and the consciousness of all souls. Therefore, the outcome can be accelerated for all. After the Winter Solstice, the New Year will take us through a cycle where Light will shine at an accelerated pace upon the planet and all souls. This will spread a new Grid of Light over the planet where darkness is no longer and evil has vanished from the face of Earth. That is the ultimate purpose of this exercise. Call for the return of the Masters of Light and the return of the Lords of Light, who are the true heirs and the caretakers of Earth and the Guardians of all Souls. Take a deep breath.

The Meditation Grid

Focus your energy on your Solar Plexus. Visualize a Ball of Bright Orange Light beginning to emanate around your belly button. Take a deep breath. Now visualize that the Ball of Light expands to reach the size of a grapefruit. Breathe into this Ball of Light until it is fully established around your waist. Through your visualization, you will be able to will this Ball of Light to form inside your Solar Plexus and to expand outward. If you have difficulty with visualization or with expression of this Ball, say, *"I call upon Jeshua to form the Orange Ball of Light around my waist and to expand it to the appropriate size on my behalf. I offer the healing benefits, the strength and power which results from this exercise in service to the Light, for the return of the Lords of Light to shine upon humankind and the planet."* Take a deep breath.

Now visualize that it expands to become the size of a pumpkin. Visualize that the same Bright Orange Ball is now super imposed upon the entire body of the planet and it extends even further to cover Earth's atmosphere, or its auric field. Bring your focus back to your own body. Breath into the pumpkin sized Orange Ball of Light and say, *"In the name of the I Am That I Am, in the name of YHWH (Yahweh), in the name of the Light of the Undifferentiated Source and the Paramatman Light, I call forth the Lords of Light to take over the guardianship of Earth and all humankind. I call forth the Seven Mighty Elohim of Light. I call forth the Archangelic Forces of Light. I call forth the presence of Divine Mother, the Feminine Principle, the Creative Force for this Universe in the form of the Goddesses of Light: Goddess Athena, Goddess Quan Yin, Goddess Hecate, Goddess of Victory, Goddess of Liberty, Mother Mary, Lady Nada, Mary Magdalene, Isis, Pele, Saraswati, Lakshmi, Durga, Kali together with the perfected presence of the I Am That I Am. I now set in motion the following decree:*

- *Annihilation of evil and all acts of evil;*
- *Release of all darkness from the bodies of Earth and all souls;*
- *Return of the Lords of Light to take guardianship of the planet and all souls."*

Visualize the pumpkin sized Ball of Light around your belly extending to become a large cocoon around your entire body. Repeat the three intentions once again. Take a deep breath and pause for a moment.

Focus on holding the energy for a few minutes by visualizing the Bright Ball of Light fully encompassing the globe and cocooning the entire planet. Now visualize yourself standing on top of the globe. Visualize a Pillar of White Light extending from the heavens above

118

down to you. This Pillar of Light is directly connected to the Seven Lords of Light. It brings in the Higher Light and the Guardianship of the Lords of Light down to the planet. It forms all around you like a Cylinder of Bright Light. It will extend through Earth and out at the other end. Pause and take a deep breath.

The Cylinder of Light will expand until the entire planet is held inside of it. The energies of the Lords of Light are moving through the Cylinder into your body and the body of Mother Earth. The Guardianship of the Lords of Light is established through you to Earth. Repeat the invocation one more time. You can do this exercise while you are sitting down, standing up or lying down. You can also invoke your Higher Self and your Guardian Angels to perform this exercise with you and on your behalf at times when you are unable to perform it yourself.

It is important that you remember the three intentions and repeat them at all times in all circumstances. It is of great benefit to you and to Earth to perform the above meditational exercise with the invocation at least once a day. The more you practice this exercise, the easier it will become to spontaneously visualize and say the invocation. The exact words are not as important as the intention.

We are setting the pace to eliminate evil and to diminish and release the hold of the dark on the body of the planet. Most importantly, we are intending to invite a much greater Force of Light and goodness to return to the planet and to take the reigns of leadership and guardianship of the planet and all souls. Peace and harmony will return to Earth and we will enjoy a greater level of closeness as the Quotient of Light increases and as more of you reach Enlightenment.

As Light replaces darkness, the Masters of Light are able to physically walk amongst us. Your prayers and intentions can make a great difference in accelerating the outcome. I urge you to choose love and compassion, Light and peace. I beckon you to set out your intentions to become the disciples of the Masters of Light and to offer yourself in service to Light at their command. It is my prayer that you would be walking by their side when that momentous experience unfolds. Join me in my prayers, that together we can experience the glory of Light and spread the victory of Light through the hands of the Lords of Light, the Masters of Light and their disciples. I hold all of you close to my heart and I pray for your victory in Light, through Light, as Light.

I am your brother Jeshua Ben Joseph. Adonai.

"I trust, I surrender, I obey, I accept."
Jeshua Ben Joseph

CHAPTER X

SHORT TERM FINANCIAL ABUNDANCE

This candle grid is for immediate manifestation of specific things, especially money. It can provide fast relief of stagnant situations and bottlenecks. It is important to realize that the biggest deterrent to manifestation can be the mind. It can get in the way and cause doubts which in turn create obstacles or delays in the process of manifestation. To help us with our doubting mind, Metatron suggests that we start with an object or an amount of money that our minds can accept as a possibility without creating doubts and obstacles. Sometimes it pays to appease the mind by going for a smaller amount or for something which the mind is not vested in.

I once gave an abundance and prosperity workshop which ran over a six week period of time. The Masters gave instructions to the workshop participants which were then followed daily by each participant at home. During the first week, the assignment was to manifest one red or yellow rose using the tools given during that first exercise. The objective was for the mind of each participant to realize that the tools given and the power of manifestation applied by each participant did indeed bring the object of desires.

At the next meeting everyone had a story to tell about how they manifested their rose. One woman had found a perfect red rose as she was getting out of her car outside her house. Another person had received a bouquet of roses as a thank-you gift from a colleague and yet another woman received roses from her husband. One man had bought a bunch of red roses for his girlfriend and she had picked one out and offered it back to him as the sign of her love for him. One person had bought a bouquet of flowers for her home as part of her weekly routine and while arranging the flowers at home realized there was a yellow rose among them. Another participant had asked her daughter to purchase a large quantity of artificial flowers to make into a garland and was delighted to see that she had bought roses. Some participants had chosen a small item for their first trial and had successfully manifested their desire.

In contrast to this, there was one person who had nothing to report. By the following week she had dropped out of the class for personal reasons. It is perfectly valid that at certain times in life we may not be ready or willing to move out of a given situation, even if our consciousness, our Higher Self or our guides choose it for us.

Some lessons we choose to learn the hard way. There can be many valid reasons for this. It may be because we learn them more thoroughly that way. It may be because in that way we remember the outcome for a longer period of time, maybe for the rest of our lives. Remaining in a position of lack and learning the lessons from it on a deeper level, is more effective in the long term than repeating the same bad habits or patterns over and over and being rescued each time by someone or through the intercession of the Masters.

On one occasion, when I set myself the task of manifesting a lump sum of money, I sent out the intention, *"Six thousand dollars over a six week period, and it is fine for the money to come in smaller increments over that period."* To which the Masters said, *"Oh, no."* Put out the intention, *"Six thousand dollars over a three week period and all at once in a lump sum."* I changed my intention and repeated the Masters' instruction with some degree of disbelief. Nevertheless, I used the manifestation technique given to me daily as instructed.

At the end of the three weeks, I had been offered a check for five thousand dollars. When I sat with myself in disbelief at how easy it had been, I realized that I really could have manifested the entire amount just as the Masters told me had my mind been a little less doubtful. Then the enthusiasm set in to make sure I continued the grid until the other one thousand had manifested. On the fourth week, two people offered me one thousand dollars each for the project I was trying to complete. One of them was the same person who had offered the first sum. Had I been trusting of my own powers of manifestation, the tools that the Masters gave me and their power of intercession on my behalf, the entire process would have proceeded more smoothly and much faster.

As you set up the Grid of Manifestation below, be watchful to catch those limiting thoughts and beliefs that the mind throws at you. You can deal with the limitation by: 1) appeasing the mind by lowering your expectation and reducing the amount to a sum your mind can accept, 2) becoming even more determined to push full force to compensate for the limitations from the mind (or its lack of participation), proving to yourself and to the mind that you can do it, 3) dealing with the limitation by working on healing all the issues which cause the mind's lack of participation, fear of success or lack of self worth.

While you are working on healing your issues, you can also try your luck with manifesting a small amount through the candle grid. This way you gain greater confidence in your own powers and the power of manifestation in the candle grid through the intercession of the Masters.

Beloveds of my own heart, I am Metatron. Take a deep breath with me.

I will give you a candle grid to manifest cash flow into your hands and your life. For this exercise, set up a tall, green candle and a tall, red candle. Pillar candles (3" x 9") are great for this grid. Place a yellow colored square piece of poster board under the candles. Draw the sign of infinity big enough so that the entire green candle sits in the left hand loop and the entire red candle sits in the right hand loop. Fill the entire sign of infinity with cinnamon, with extra room between the candle and the edge of the sign. As you draw the sign, very emphatically say, *"Cash in hand now in the name of the I Am That I Am, immediately. Cash in my hands immediately."* Repeat this statement over and over again until you have finished the entire set-up process for this grid. Draw it first with gold colored pen and then cover the gold with the cinnamon. The cinnamon is encapsulating each candle.

Draw a diamond shaped rectangle around the sign of infinity. The point starts in the north and goes to the east, down to the south, then west, then back to the north. The sign of infinity sits inside of the diamond. The green candle is positioned in the west and the red in the east. Draw a circle around the diamond so that the four points of the diamond touch the edge of the circle. The diamond represents the connection of this mundane realm of reality to the Higher Realms where instant manifestation is truly instant. The circle represents the realm where time and space are no longer separated; there is instant manifestation within the time-space continuum.

Metratron's Grid for Short Term Finances

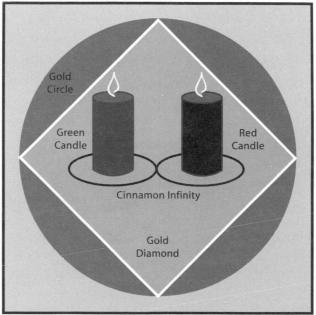

Yellow Poster Board

This is the strongest manifestation grid that I have as yet given to any one of you. I want you to be very specific and make just the one intention, for example say, *"Fifty thousand dollars to manifest in my hands right now."* If your mind cannot accept that amount, then do not ask for that amount. Your mind must get out of the way and accept this as possible. It must surrender. If your mind cannot believe you can manifest fifty thousand dollars, start with a smaller amount. Once you have manifested it, start the candle grid again with a larger amount.

Doubt and disbelief are great deterrents to the manifestation process. It is better to begin with an amount which your mind is willing to work with and does not object to. Targeting smaller amounts over a shorter span of time may be more acceptable to your mind. Then the mind will not get in your way and will cooperate in the manifestation process. Light your candles at least once daily or as many times as you can, and say the intention over and over until you manifest the amount you intended. Once you manifest that amount, start again with a larger amount. Do this over and over again each time with a greater number, and do not stop until you have gained enough momentum, strength and power that you can continue to manifest regularly without the need of the candle grid. If the process slows down or if you feel you are being distracted or losing focus, go back and start a new round with the candle grid.

It is important to keep the momentum and heighten your focus and intention as well as the frequency of repetition. The more you focus, the greater the outcome. The more you say the invocation with force and command, the faster the manifestation becomes. I wish you great joy and success in this endeavor.

I am your father, Metatron.

Summary

Materials needed:

- Yellow poster board cut to a 12" square

- Two 3" x 9" pillar candles — one green, one red

- Gold-ink marker, gel or felt pen

- Ruler and protractor or 10"-11" plate (to draw circle)

- Cinnamon

Instructions for creating the Candle Grid

1. At each step and for the entire time you are making this grid say, *"Cash at hand now in the name of the I Am That I Am. Cash in my hands immediately."*

2. On the yellow poster board, with a gold pen, draw an equilateral diamond with 6" sides. Start in the north drawing down to the east, then south, then west, and then back to the north.

3. Place the 2 candles in the diamond; green candle on the left (west), red candle on the right (east).

4. Inside the diamond and around the candles, draw the sign of infinity with the cinnamon, large enough for each candle to sit inside a loop with extra space around it. You may draw the sign first with the gold pen then cover it with the cinnamon.

5. Draw a circle of gold around the diamond so that the four points of the diamond touch the edge of the circle.

6. Say the mantras and follow the instructions in the text in order to imbue the unlighted candles and when lighting each of the candles.

7. Light your candles with your one specific intention as many times a day as you can, and say the mantra over and over until you manifest the amount you had intended.

CHAPTER XI

DISCIPLES OF CHRIST MAITREYA

In honor of the auspicious holiday of Thanksgiving, which is celebrated in November, beloved Master Jeshua Ben Joseph offers us the opportunity of taking a vow of discipleship and to merge with Christ Maitreya. I hope that you enjoy this meditational journey. Allow yourself to contemplate Jeshua's simple message and repeat this like a mantra with every breath.

"I trust, I surrender, I obey and I accept."

Jesus tells us with these four qualities we can move mountains. Enjoy these auspicious days which are the harbinger of great unity and acceleration on the path of Enlightenment. Jesus calls upon a host of angels. Among these, Archangel Ratziel, who is the Guardian of the Crown Chakra and Sandalphon, the Guardian of the Root Chakra. Uriel, Raphael, Michael and Gabriel are the Angelic Forces of the Four Directions and together with Chamiel, Zadkiel and Jophiel, they make the Seven Archangelic Forces of the Seven Rays. Azriel is the Guardian of the Dead and Samael guards our darkness. For more on Archangels read *Path to Enlightenment, Book II* and *Gifts from the Masters of Light: Journeys Into the Inner Realms of Consciousness — Gifts III,* by Nasrin Safai.

Adonai, Beloveds I am Jeshua Ben Joseph.

Focus all your attention in the center of your heart. I call forth the energies of Christ Maitreya and the hierarchies of the Masters of Wisdom who walk with him. I, Jeshua Ben Joseph, represent the Christ energies for Earth. I offer myself to become the bridge between Christ Maitreya and the human beings of Earth. I call forth our Lord Metatron and the Angelic Forces of Michael, Uriel, Raphael, Gabriel, Chamuel, Ratziel, Zadkiel, Sandalphon, Azriel, Jophiel and Samael to be present with us.

In the name of the Lords of Light and in service to the Light, we ask the presence of Christ Maitreya to dissolve the veil which separates the consciousness of humankind from the Divine Universal Consciousness. Now open your heart and pour a shower of blessings, love and Light from to these Angelic Forces, for they will play an important role in the unfolding of events for Earth and humankind.

Presently, the energies of the Cobalt Blue Light are emanating from the God-Source at the inner core of the galaxy to all the planets in this solar system. The sun is receiving and filtering these energies. To cope with these energies, it is important that you become harmonious within yourself and tune in to the rhythm of these energies. This Cobalt Blue Light has its own beat and rhythm. Once you learn to tune into these energies, you can benefit from their Divine Harmony. When you awaken in the morning, envision that a blanket of Cobalt Blue Light is enfolding you. Visualize that the surface of your skin is immersed in this Light. The vibration and the rhythm of this new energy is different; so different that it may throw you off balance. Do not be concerned if you feel dizzy, nauseous, or have pressure headaches, agitation, anxiety, panic, pain or any other experience of discomfort. This is a temporary phase. The Cobalt Blue Light will heighten your rhythm in harmony with its own beat. Then you will be expanded to grow spiritually and feel a closer affinity with these Divine Energies. Take a deep breath.

By visualizing yourself wrapped inside of the God-Source vibration of Cobalt Blue Light, you will be capable of receiving energies through the surface of your skin. You will absorb, digest and process these energies and begin to act from a space of receptivity. Then, when you notice that the energy is moving through you, you will receive and welcome it willingly rather than feel burdened and concerned.

As you practice calling upon the Cobalt Blue Light and immersing yourself in its powerful Light, your experience of the presence of the Masters of Wisdom and Light become more tangible and the impact of the energies more potent. You may gradually build upon your ability to experience the range of the spectrum which this Cobalt Blue Light covers. However, at first it may seem as though you take two steps forward and one step back. Be patient while this is becoming a new dance, until you get used to the rhythm of these new energies. When this rhythm becomes part of your beingness, you will no longer have to take one step back. You will take a sequence of two steps forward and a pause, and then again two steps forward. In this way the rhythm becomes easier to follow, and the pace faster. At this greater pace of acceleration, there are things that you will have to push aside to move forward. Your heart, mind, soul and your spirit would urge the consciousness of your body to move forward. The universe will open up the doors, and the golden gateways of spiritual growth will usher you to move further forward in those directions without any further delays.

Vow to be in the Discipleship of Christ Maitreya

Take a moment now and go deep within the stillness of your heart. I will offer you a prayer of invocation, a vow to accelerate you to the Attainment of God-Unity. Repeat this vow with your consciousness, your heart, mind, body, emotions, soul and spirit. Say this vow,

"I vow that I will never be delayed by anyone, anything, any place, any distraction, any obstacle on my path of accelerating to God-Unity. I vow that I will never consciously stand in anyone's way of accelerating on this path. I request that if, consciously or unconsciously, I have become the instrument for delay for anyone that they now be released from my obstruction. I request that if anyone becomes the instrument of delay for me, that they be removed from my path and I removed from theirs. I ask that we all continue to accelerate at the pace best suited to our needs. I ask for support from the universe through the Masters of Wisdom, Masters of Light and the Angelic Forces of Light. I ask that I may continue to walk upon this path at

the accelerated pace set before me. I ask for my nervous system to be strengthened that I may be able to withstand the intensity of the accelerated pace. I ask that my mind, my consciousness, my emotions and my body be strengthened to withstand and to enjoy every moment of walking on this path at an accelerated pace.

I ask those amongst the Masters of Light and Wisdom who are my guides, guardians, Masters, friends, older brothers and sisters, to come forward and to teach me. I am ready to be the disciple, the student, the practitioner, to the Masters. I allow myself to be set on the path of Enlightenment at an accelerated pace. I offer myself in service to the Light through these Masters. I ask for assistance, guidance, protection, love, sustenance, Life Force, Light, abundance, strength, courage, fearlessness, surrender, mercy, compassion, patience and perseverance to engulf me."

"I ask for support from all levels and dimensions of reality through members of my own Soul Lineage. I offer my support for members of my own Soul Lineage; I vow to become the bridge to connect the old world and the old ways to the new world and the new ways to reach God-Unity at a greater pace. I vow to become the bridge for the multitudes and masses to cross from the abyss of ignorance and forgetfulness to the haven of Light, love, self realization and God-Unity. I offer what remains of this lifetime (and however many more lifetimes may be necessary) for the continuation of this intention until it bears fruit."

"To achieve all that I have requested, I seek discipleship of the Masters. I ask for the ability to withstand the Light of the World Teacher and to be in His physical presence. I ask for all dross, pain, suffering, fears, lack, limitations, ego, arrogance, and duality which remain within me to fall away and be released from me. I ask to be purified and brought back to the perfection necessary to withstand the Light of Christ Maitreya and His physical presence. I ask for the clearing and cleansing to commence from this moment on and to expand and accelerate at the pace most suitable for me."

"I surrender and I stand in the presence of the Angelic Forces mentioned above. I vow to serve Master Jesus (Jeshua), Christ Maitreya and all the Masters of Light and Wisdom who will make this endeavor possible. I vow for all that I gain to be offered in their service and for the benefit of the multitudes and masses. I seek acceleration in raising of the consciousness of the multitudes and masses and the awakening of all souls to their true Divine Spark."

"On behalf of the souls who choose to remain unaware, I ask for a speedy mass migration to realms of reality where they can find their happiness. On behalf of the souls who are pioneers on this path, I ask for strength and courage to spearhead the plan of acceleration. I offer myself in whatever way I may be of greatest service. I open my heart seeking to be contented, joyous, accepting and grateful, for whatever part I may play in the great scheme of this great Divine Plan. I trust, I surrender, I obey, and I accept my acceleration on the path of Enlightenment." Now take a deep breath.

MEDITATION TO MERGE WITH CHRIST MAITREYA

See yourself wrapped in the blanket of Cobalt Blue Light. Visualize yourself standing inside a circle under a Pillar of Light. Visualize Cobalt Blue Light pouring down to this circle. Feel the energy as it moves around the circle. In the Light of the I Am That I Am, I, Jeshua Ben Joseph, call forth the presence of my Lord, Christ Maitreya, to the center of this circle. Visualize Christ Maitreya walking to stand in front of you. He is tall and broad shouldered. He is emanating the Teal Blue-Green color which is his special signature. Allow yourself to be immersed in Light. Allow your heart to synchronize in rhythm with the Force of His presence standing in the middle of your circle.

If you begin to experience sharp pains especially in the region of the head, know this to be an expansion. Sharp pains in the back of the neck between the shoulder blades or in lower back are signs of opening specific chakras which play an important role in the acceleration process. Feel the presence of Christ Maitreya with you. In this auspicious moment where His presence is felt in your heart and in your own auric field, ask Him for whatever you desire. Request him to give you specific or general, personal or global intentions for yourself, your loved ones and for the multitudes and masses. Seek and you shall find. Knock and it shall be opened to you. Ask and you shall receive. Ask now. Know that He hears your every thought. Know that He is with you when called upon with every breath. Know that He will stay for as long as you ask Him to. He has taken this time to be in service to all of you.

Those of you who call upon Him and have made an effort to experience and know His presence take precedence over those who are as yet un-awakened and insensitive to His presence. With this exercise and others like it, your consciousness becomes receptive to His presence. Therefore, you become the anchor for His energies on Earth. When He comes to exchange energies with you, you will benefit from His presence. He too will benefit from your presence, for through your presence He can reach out to the multitudes and masses. He therefore welcomes every opportunity to be called by you to allow the anchoring of His energies in your auric field and your chakras. Fully immerse yourself in His presence and ask from the core of your heart for whatever desires and intentions you wish to manifest. Pause and take a few deep breaths.

Christ Maitreya beckons you to join Him to merge and unite in His energies; to surrender to His presence and His Light. Allow your consciousness to dissolve inside of His presence. Your consciousness will merge and unite into His and your ego-personality will dissolve. You will become a drop from the ocean that He is. Take a deep breath and pause.

Ask that all mundane level entanglements, karmic or otherwise, be released. Ask that you may focus your energies, attention and all your resources on serving and assisting Him to guide the multitudes and masses to greater consciousness of Light and to the ultimate goal of God-Unity. Seek to release all those issues, events, circumstances, people, relationships, plans, programs, and things that you are attached to. Believe that they no longer have a grip on you. See His influence dissolve all your attachments and all fears. Ask for deep surrender to and acceptance of your Divine Mission. Ask for the grace to reach complete acceptance of your mission, as part of his own mission,

Call now to all members of your own Soul Lineage to join and merge inside this Pillar of Light with you and into the presence of Christ Maitreya. In this way you will accelerate both your own journey on the path of Light and theirs. Your Soul Lineage consists of those individuals who are your own soul family members. Their souls and yours originate from the same source. The forces of every member of your Soul Lineage are added to your own as they join and merge with you. You are offering them an opportunity to reach higher goals and attain those goals along with you. You will provide them with the ability to seek greater goals and to see those goals as attainable. Seek the attainment of those goals in the presence of Christ Maitreya. Stand in His Light and hold the hem of His robes, invoke Him to give you the object of your desires. Do not let go until you know in the core of your heart that He has given it to you. Ask Him to give these desires or better, as He sees fit.

Repeat this exercise at least once a day for twenty two days. If you miss a day, continue the following day and add a day at the end to complete the twenty two.

People, places or things may be in need of your prayers. Add them to your prayers. As people reach greater consciousness, they let go of their inhibitions and fears, dogmatic beliefs and traditions and separate themselves from the mainstream. Pray specifically for the consciousness of these layers of the society; the ones who set themselves apart and consider themselves *"The Chosen Ones."* They may be isolating themselves and moving into dogmatic thoughts and behaviors. It is for these layers of society that we need to pray the most. Those who do not know and are asleep can be awakened. Those who have already been awakened and are following the path are already on their path. The hardest ones are those who refuse to see what is ahead of them because of their self imposed preconceived notions and dogmatic ideas.

Through this exercise, Christ Maitreya and the Masters of Wisdom can accelerate focusing their energies physically here on Earth. The five elements benefit from His presence on Earth. This is another reason why the veil is lifting. The veil is connected to the consciousness of the multitudes and masses. It is also connected to the vibration of the four Base Elements: the Earth, Water, Air and Fire.

The Fifth Element, Ether, is sublime and holds all the other elements within it. The element of Ether does not become contaminated. It is the Four Lower Elements which become polluted or contaminated. They cause the personality and the consciousness to act accordingly, even when such actions are against your principles. By bathing yourself in His presence and by calling His presence to your side, you will purify the Four Lower Elements and elevate them to hold Higher Light.

Remember to remain in joy and in gratitude. One of the most sublime of emotions is the vibration of gratitude. Compassion, mercy, and love are all components of the ultimate goal. Gratitude is the crowning glory. With gratitude empires can be built. Remember that gratitude must go hand in hand with acceptance; not blind-folded acceptance, but premeditated acceptance; acceptance which leads you to surrender, and surrender which results in gratitude, every time. This is the formula: acceptance leads to surrender, surrender brings with it gratitude, for where there is surrender there is acceptance. There are no exceptions. Where there are no expectations, every action, every thought, every movement would lead you to greater gratitude. Remember it is importance to create a greater solid foundation in every relationship, interaction, event or circumstance. If you are building a high rise building, you have to dig deeper into the ground to create a solid foundation strong enough to support forty, fifty or seventy stories. The same applies to relationships.

Remember: trust, surrender, obedience, acceptance and gratitude must become your mantra, *"I trust, I surrender, I obey, I accept."* Make this your mantra. In this phase of acceleration, you have a large window of opportunity. Remember the magic, the magic of these four qualities: *"I trust, I surrender, I obey, I accept."* If you truly believe in these four qualities, you will be unstoppable.

At this auspicious time I hold each one of you with great joy in my own heart. I bless you in all your endeavors and I walk with you along this path. It is with great jubilation and celebration that I bid you farewell.

I am Jeshua Ben Joseph. So it is.

CHAPTER XII

GODDESS HECATE, QUAN YIN, ARCHANGEL MICHAEL AND METATRON

Goddess Hecate, Lady Quan Yin, Archangel Michael, and Metatron bid us into the energies of the New Year with love, joy and celebration. From the 9th to the 19th of January of every year, there is a Portal of Energy open which brings Light from the constellation of Sirius. Planets from this constellation are believed to be the parents of the present seed race of humankind on Earth. Great work can be done to accelerate us on our path during this time.

Archangel Michael offers us the Ankh of Power which is one of the power objects popular with Syrian Gods and Goddesses, especially Isis and Osiris. Michael offers this energetic Ankh to empower you to the memories of the power and might prevalent on Earth during the early years of the civilization of Khem, the land where Egypt is today. The tombs and pyramids of Egypt bear witness to what remains of the ancient civilization built by our ancestors from Sirius.

Metatron reminds us to trust, Quan Yin requests that we wear pearls through December and January and Goddess Hecate calls for the energies of turquoise. Pearls relieve the pressure of pain and struggle. Turquoise expels negative energies from our auric field. It also prevents any external negativity from seeping into our energy field.

My Children, I am Hecate.

I offer each one of you the fiery opal encased in a ring of black obsidian and place this directly behind your naval in the area of your Solar Plexus. This is the center for power. It is also the place where your energy can be leaked or depleted. Energy is extended as well as received, and power can be exchanged from here. The fiery opal will give you the fire, the zest, the fervor and the Life Force with which to grab and hold on to what duly belongs to you. It will not allow anyone to take from you what is rightfully yours. The black obsidian is to hold you grounded in the power and to help you know what is rightly yours. Use it to better yourself, your life, and the lives of others and to serve the multitudes and masses. Obsidian is a stone which is made of lava from volcanic eruptions. It comes out from the heart of Goddess Pele, The Goddess of Volcanoes. So too is the fiery opal. The fiery opal is the love of a mother for her child. I give you this gem, which is an alchemical tool to bring you power to absorb and use the acceleration which is coming to you and to turn the chaos, which is here now, into joyful and positive change. Chaos brings about change. Therefore, chaos should be enjoyed. Change always follows chaos and change should be welcomed. When you have the wisdom to see the change as a tool for improving yourself and the power to turn the chaos to favorable change, then what fear have you? None.

My prayer for you is to see you as wise, fearless, glorious, victorious, mighty and empowered. My prayer for you, my children, is to be successful; to have it all and to not be attached to it, to know that everything is transitory. Things can go in the same way that they came and they can come back again. My prayer is that you are empowered long enough to manifest all your desires and to know how to use what you have to benefit yourself and others. My prayer is to love yourself enough to want the best for yourself and trust the world enough to give it away again and again and again, knowing it will come back to you tenfold, a hundred fold, a thousand fold, over and over again.

I hold all of you in my own bosom. I will nurture you, I will cherish you, I will teach you, I will help you, and I will walk with you and show you the way. I am your Mother Hecate. It is a pleasure to see you walk on this path and be glorious. It is my intention to walk with you and see you to victory and share your glory. Do not forget your Mother Hecate in times of high and low. I treat all my mighty children with great love. I treat all my obedient children with great sustenance and abundance. Those who disobey and abuse will be punished. There is no other way. Even though chaos is the mother of change, those who create chaos for no reason at all will pay the price for the chaos that they create. That is the law of the universe. And those who see the chaos and stay in the eye of the whirlwind with no fears will come out of the hurricane unscathed. I will stand by your side. I will show you the way. I will make you proud.

I am your mother, Hecate. So it is.

My Beloved Children, I am Quan Yin.

I have come to all of you with a great open heart and much love. I do have one request. We are entering a time of transition which will last through December until the 19th of January. This will bring great acceleration and changes in your lives. I wish to ask you to wear pearls during this time of acceleration. Also, please know that Goddess Hecate has requested that you wear turquoise. The pearls will balance the turquoise. The turquoise will help to dislodge pain and dross from your body. What the turquoise pulls out, the pearls will soften up and release. As the pains come up, the pearls can take the pains away in a gentle way. Make a point of wearing pearls with any other gems: turquoise, rubies, obsidian, platinum, gold or silver. Wear pearls at all times to the end of January.

The energies for clearing of your emotional and mental bodies can be accelerated with these gems. During this time of the year, you can feel the power of acceleration. Ride this tide because it will put you on a different plateau which is a pleasant place to be. The energy of anxiety may come up. Ride that energy too. See it as positive and helpful. See it as a means to release uncertainty and the fear of the unknown from your cell structure. Change is about to happen in many directions. Always welcome change. With change you will grow to become wise. You will begin to see yourself from the position of a witness. You will begin to accept yourself for whom you are and agree to change those aspects of your own behavior, which no longer serve you, in order to move forward. I support you with all of my heart. Energy of opal is also beneficial at this time. It will bring you wisdom. Opal is the equivalent of the old wise woman/man who has lived a fruitful life and has helped many and has finally been recognized. Opals will help to bring you wisdom. Opals help you to vibrate to the new upcoming energies and in rhythm with the vibration of Earth.

I hold you with great love in my own heart as all of you are my own children. I love you. I cherish you. I nurture you. Call upon me. I am here by your side.

I am your mother, Quan Yin.

My Brethren of Light, I am Michael

I have come on this auspicious day to offer you the energies of the Ankh of Power. I have brought these energies with the objective to empower you. The power is given in the form of an ankh. Visualize an ankh illuminated with Golden Platinum colors. Tongues of fire are beaming from the circular arc of the ankh.

Ankh

I will place it around your neck by standing behind you. I will place the circular arc over your head. The cross will fit over your chest, from one shoulder to the other and the length of the cross will cover you all the way to your Root Chakra. Visualize this Ankh of Power. The presence of this ankh is to energize you with the power you need for these accelerated times. With the use of the Ankh of Power, you will have the strength, the stamina, and the courage to use this phase of acceleration to the utmost of your ability. The objective is to reach the highest and the ultimate point of growth on the path of Enlightenment and in service to humankind. It is important that you have success; it is important that you have financial abundance; it is important that you have peace of mind; and it is important that you are able to harness your emotions. Harnessing your emotions helps you stabilize your emotional body. This means you can have joy in your heart and gratitude in your mind at all times, under all circumstances.

Visualize Archangel Michael standing behind you and receive the Ankh of Power. Take a deep breath and pause to integrate the power from the Ankh. I wish you great success in all your endeavors,

I am your brother, Michael.

Beloveds of my own heart, I am Metatron. Take a deep breath.

As the beginning of a new year approaches, let us together celebrate everyday in gratitude, trust, love and in surrender. Obedience comes when there is love and surrender mixed with trust. Obedience is a word that runs shivers along the back of many, yet obedience comes easily to those who have trust, surrender and love. Receive the love that comes to you from the Higher Realms and know that you have all paid your dues. The gateways of mercy open up to bring Light and dark together. Each one of you have agreed to be a participant in the task of bringing Light and dark together.

To this end you have allowed your own physical bodies, emotional bodies, mental bodies, and spiritual bodies to be the catalyst, the conduit, the antenna, through which these energies can unite. When you have such an agreement in place and truly believe in it, then neither of these two opposing factions (Light and Dark) would feel threatened by you. They would consider you an ally. Therefore you will have no obstacles on the path of success, abundance, relationships, wisdom, career, or spiritual growth.

You live in the world of duality. In such a world, Light and Dark are responsible for weaving the tapestry of existence together. By overlooking the presence of darkness you would be ignoring or denying what really goes on in this third dimensional reality. Those who are successful are the ones that consciously or subconsciously take account of this fact. Now without taking sides and without drowning yourself in drama of the battle of Light and dark, begin to come to that place of neutrality where you are wiling to understand and accept that through you, the Light and Dark may unite. Actively allow this union to take place inside of you. Your choice to follow and promote the Light is great and righteous. However, stay nonjudgmental and respectful of the presence of darkness and accept it as a part of the present fabric of your reality. By accepting it, you can do something to release it. By denying its presence, you are unconsciously holding onto it.

This third dimensional reality has two sides to it. One side is Dark, the other side is Light. If you were looking at a coin you would not have an issue with the head or the tail side. You would simply accept that head denotes one side and tail the other. Both sides live in harmony with each other and are inseparable.

Remember that you can choose joy. You have the choice to see an event as an obstacle or as a means to redirect you, perhaps to take a short cut. You can see the situation as an obstacle on your path, delaying you, or as a means for greater growth, wisdom and understanding. I suggest you seek to know the reason why you feel stuck. You will not feel stuck, or confront obstacles unless it is leading you to something greater, faster, easier, and more enjoyable.

Consciously seek ways to bring you acceleration, joy, celebration, gratitude, happiness, abundance, and positive attitude. It is fun to wake up everyday and know that you are provided for. It is fun to do what you do out of love not out of obligation. The time has come for you to know that your dues are paid. Therefore, what remains is reaping the harvest. Reap the harvest. Be contented and know that you have earned it. Remind yourself that you have earned it, not with arrogance, but with humility; always be righteous. Demand and command that the universe will provide you with joy, gratitude, comfort, and luxury. Comfort and luxury are two of my favorite things. Make your goal comfort, luxury, harmony, peace and gratitude.

I hold you with great joy in my own heart. I stand at your feet with folded arms as your own father Metatron, El-Shaddai. So it is.

*"If you do nothing but remember what I have taught you, everyday,
you have blessed me, the Divine Mother, all the Masters
and you have served the Light.*

*Do what you can when you can and know that we all hold you in our hearts,
In the presence of all the Thrones, The Feminine Creative Force manifest as
Quan Yin, Hecate, Isis, Pele, Athena, Nada, Victory, Liberty, Lakshmi,
Saraswati, Durga, Kali, Mother Mary and Christ Maitreya, Jesus,
Sanat Kumara, St. Germain, Melchizedeck, Ancient of Days, Thoth,
Cosmic and Great Beings of Light, Brotherhoods and the Sisterhoods
of the White Lodge, the Seven Mighty Elohim, the Seven Chohan,
the Seven Lords of Light and the Maha Lord of Light.*

I bid you farewell and I hold you in my own heart. So it is."

Metatron
September 9, 2008

CHANNELING INDEX

Chapter IV: Ascension Day and Paramatman
Preparation for Paramatman Light
and 1,000 Years of Peace; 24th of April,
Ascension Day for Humanity
- Used in April 2006 Newsletter
- Metatron, channeled February 24, 2005

Chapter V: Protection
Cocoon of Protection for Healers
- Used in May 2006 Newsletter
- Mother Mary, channeled August 26, 2004

Chapter VI: Healing, Compassion and Mercy
Grid of Healing, Compassion and Mercy with
Guardian Angels of Intellect and Emotion and
Archangel Uriel, Raphael, and Michael
- Quan Yin, channeled December 9, 2005

Chapter VII: Financial Abundance and Relationships
Candle Grid for Financial Abundance
and Relationships
- Used in June 2006 Newsletter
- Quan Yin, channeled September 1, 2004

Chapter VIII: 1st, 2nd and 3rd Levels of Initiation
Meditation to Receive the 1st, 2nd and 3rd Levels
of Initiation from Christ Maitreya
- Christ Maitreya, channeled through Metatron
  July 24, 2008

BIBLIOGRAPHY

Bailey, Alice. *Initiation Human and Solar.* Lucias Publishing Co., 1997.

Bailey, Alice. *Rays and Initiations: A Treatise on the Seven Rays (Rays and the Initiations).* Lucias Publishing Co., 1960.

Crème, Benjamin. *Maitreya's Mission Vol. I & II.* Share International Foundation, 2002.

McClure, Jane. *Sanat Kumara: Training a Planetary Logos (Tools for Transformation).* Light Technology Publishing, 1990.

Meera, Mother. *Answers Part I.* Mother Meera Publications, Germany, 1991.

Peterson, Wayne S. *Extraordinary Times, Extraordinary Beings: Experiences of an American Diplomat with Maitreya and the Masters of Wisdom.* Hampton Roads Publishing Company, 2003.

Szekely, Edmond-Bordeaux. *Essene Gospel of Peace, Vol. I, II, III, IV.* International Biogenic Society, 1981.

Szekely, Edmond-Bordeaux. *The Essence Science of Light, According to the Essene Gospel of Peace.* International Biogenic Society, 1986.

ORGANIZATION WEBSITES FOR RELATED INFORMATION

www.karunamayi.org
www.mmdarshanamerica.com
www.waynepeterson.com
www.path-to-enlightenment.com
www.nasrinsafai.com

www.amma.org
www.share-international.org
www.yantradesigngroup.com
www.godunity.org
www.wavesofbliss.com

ACKNOWLEDGEMENTS

*I offer thanks to all beings and all people
who have contributed to bring these books to life.*

With great love, I thank the following people for their contributions.

*To Patsy Balacchi of Yantra Design Group, for cover design,
photography, typography, and her enthusiasm and zest for perfection.*

To Jane A. Matthews for her publishing and editing skills.

*To James Foster and editing team members Tonia Pinhiero, Kathy Rowshan
and Susie Farley. To Michael Kopel, our technical support chief,
Theresa Martin for diagram design, and James Foster for original drawings.*

To Tom Campell of King Printing and Adi Books.

*For invaluable comments and editing remarks, I thank Jeffery Foster,
Allen Blanchard, Hara Weaver, Kathy Roshan and Tonia Pinhiero.*

To Dr. John Alderson and Shabnam Sadr for their loving support.

*Finally, I thank everyone who contributed by participating in
channeling sessions where we received the information contained in this book.*

ABOUT THE AUTHOR

Nasrin is an internationally known channel of the Ascended Masters and Angelic Beings of Light. In 1999, Lord Metatron requested of Nasrin to conduct channeled life readings to aid those souls who are drawn to find their life's mission and to recall their lineage of Light.

Part of her life's mission is to travel the world anchoring ascension energies of Light at locations on all continents through ceremonies, sacred dances, mantras, prayers and invocations given by the Masters. Nasrin has been a channel for Metatron, Melchizedek, Sanat Kumara, Archangel Michael, Uriel, Raphael, Jesus, Mother Mary, Buddha, St. Germain, Quan Yin, Hecate, Athena, Red Feather and other Ascended Beings of Light.

She attended Chelsea School of Art in London, received a Bachelors Degree from the University of Decorative Arts in Tehran, a Masters Degree in Environmental Planning from Nottingham University in England and did her Doctoral Studies in the role of women in the development of the third world. She has taught at Harvard University and universities and institutes of higher education around the world. Presently she holds the post of Professor of Esoteric Spirituality at Universal Seminary, where materials from her books are taught for college credit.

Nasrin is the founder of the Foundation for the Attainment of God-Unity (FAGU), an educational and holistic healing organization which provides classes, workshops, books and support materials for spiritual practice open to all. All proceeds from the sale of this book support the work of the Masters through FAGU (www.godunity.org).

avatars p.3
massinsafai.com